WHO ORDERED THE UNIVERSE?

WHO ORDERED THE UNIVERSE?

EVIDENCE FOR GOD IN UNEXPECTED PLACES

NICK HAWKES

MONARCH
BOOKS

Oxford UK, and Grand Rapids, USA

Published by Monarch Books
an imprint of
Lion Hudson plc
Wilkinson House, Jordan Hill Road,
Oxford OX2 8DR, England
Email: monarch@lionhudson.com
www.lionhudson.com/monarch

ISBN 978 0 85721 598 7
e-ISBN 978 0 85721 599 4

First edition 2015

Acknowledgments
Scripture quotations taken from the Holy Bible, New International Version
Anglicised. Copyright © 1979, 1984, 2011 Biblica, formerly International Bible
Society. Used by permission of Hodder & Stoughton Ltd, an Hachette UK
company. All rights reserved. "NIV" is a registered trademark of Biblica. UK
trademark number 1448790.
pp. 26–27: Extract from "Taking Science on Faith" by Paul Davies from *The New
York Times* copyright © 2007, Paul Davies. Reprinted by permission of *The New
York Times* and PARS International Corporation.
p. 208: Extract from God in the Dock by C. S. Lewis copyright © C. S. Lewis Pte.
Ltd. 1970. Reprinted by permission of The C. S. Lewis Company.

Mandelbrot Set images copyright © Wolfgang Beyer/Wikimedia Commons

A catalogue record for this book is available from the British Library

Printed and bound in UK, June 2015, LH26

To Isaac, my grandson…
that he might learn to wonder
and seek truth

CONTENTS

ACKNOWLEDGMENTS

All books are a team effort, and this is certainly the case for this book.

My heartfelt thanks goes to Greg Denholm, my friend and editor. I would be lost without his care for detail.

Mary, my wife, has been my champion, my second editor, and the one who has ensured that this work is accessible to those without specialist knowledge.

I was fortunate to secure the help of Professor Michael Clapper, who rescued me from the worst excesses of mathematical folly. Michael heads up the board of the Australian Mathematics Trust based at the University of Canberra.

My friend, Dr Leonard Long, helped me understand the intrigues surrounding the Galileo trial. He has a fine mind.

Chris and Naomi McPeake, together with Mark and Colleen White, have been the prayer team for this project. It is fabulous for any Christian author to have such people behind them providing spiritual support.

Professor David Wilkinson (Principal of St John's College, Durham University) has a gracious character and a magnificent intellect. He began this project by introducing me to Monarch Books – and taught me to trust God for the results.

Finally, I owe a huge debt of thanks to Tony Collins (Publisher for Monarch Books and Lion Fiction) who never stopped believing in me.

Nick Hawkes

FOREWORD

Revd Professor David Wilkinson

BSc, PhD MA, PhD, FRAS

Professor David Wilkinson is an astrophysicist and theologian. He is the current principal of St John's College and a professor in the Department of Theology and Religion at Durham University.

I have always been fascinated by evidence. My first school science project in the 1970s was trying to test the then fashionable claims of extrasensory perception – from bending spoons to predicting symbols on cards. The results were inevitably less exciting than the claims! Then, at a slightly more advanced level, the evidence for the bending of light by gravity… and the energy distribution of electrons ejected from a surface bathed in radiation. This introduced me to the strange worlds of relativity and quantum theory. Here evidence led to the exciting realization that the world of everyday common sense was very different to how the universe actually is. In my work as an astrophysicist, models of galaxy evolution depended on the evidence of gamma rays, radio waves, and infrared radiation. Indeed, the model of the Big Bang itself was both supported and challenged by evidence collected over decades in the twentieth century.

Yet the gathering of evidence does not easily result in scientific answers. Galileo did not point his telescope at the moons of Jupiter and immediately receive a computer printout saying, "The earth is not at the centre of the universe." Every research scientist knows that evidence has to be critically assessed. Models that interpret the evidence have to be imagined, constructed, and tested. The weight of evidence for a proposed model then has to be judged. It takes both courage and faith to send your work off to be probed and questioned by the rest of the scientific community.

Such a process is not a million miles away from my experience of becoming a Christian. I was intrigued by the awe I experienced at discovering the order of the universe. The other thing that intrigued me was the "something else" that Christian people seemed to have in their lives – something they attributed to the life, death, and resurrection of Jesus of Nazareth. I needed to explore the evidence behind this... and risk uncovering something I might have to act upon. But what is the best way to interpret this evidence... and does its weight point to the Christian picture of a God who desires to not simply be an intellectual explanation but to be in personal loving relationship with men and women? And finally, what does this mean for how I live my life today?

Since the age of seventeen, I have been shaped, challenged, and sustained by this evidence as I have attempted to follow Jesus. Faith for me is trust on the basis of evidence... which leads to action. The truth of Christianity cannot be proved, for at its heart is a personal God, not a mathematical equation. However, this does not mean that faith is irrational or so personal that it cannot be examined with reason, in the context of a conversation.

Nick Hawkes invites us into such a conversation. This book is not about proving God but is an invitation to consider a wide range of evidence that gives clues to the meaning, purpose, and value of both the universe and human life. It does so in a way that allows the best conversations to develop. Here is a conversation partner who is engaging, passionate, knowledgeable, and yet gracious in respecting the other. From his extensive experience of science, theology, and life, he invites us to examine the evidence.

He does not impose simplistic answers, nor does he dodge the difficult questions.

He represents superbly the God who has revealed evidence of his love and power... but wants to be in an enriching and intimate conversation with all men and women. It is a conversation that is both life enhancing and life changing.

INTRODUCTION

What you believe is important. It is not incidental. Your beliefs define you and form your identity. They may even be something for which you are prepared to die. Your beliefs are a sacred thing... so, let me make you this promise: I shall tread gently in the places where you let me wander.

With this assurance, let me invite you to explore with me whether belief in God is reasonable. Has God left clues about his existence in the universe?

As we begin this journey, I am driven by a conviction that I find both disturbing and intimidating. It is this: Only the truth is worthy of you – so I must be careful.

Taking care with the truth means we can't just accept everything as being right. It is not the case that we can believe whatever we like, provided we are nice to people. That is simply giving up the search for truth. Being good to others is a belief that can only have meaning if we know what authentic "good" is. Otherwise, being "good" is not really good. It is just the most convenient and efficient way for most of us to get along. Fundamentally, it is an expression of the self-interest of the majority.

It is tempting in these days of political correctness to be deeply suspicious of any religion or philosophy that claims to have a handle on truth. Today's mantra is "everything must be tolerated".

To say this, however, is to capitulate to evil. It gives the worst abuses of religion the power to prevent you from searching for spiritual meaning, and it allows those abuses to be tolerated. Some religions and philosophies should not be tolerated. "Honour killings" (a dreadfully inappropriate name), the execution of those who convert to another faith, suicide bombers... these things should be named for what they are: evil.

The problem is, as soon as we do that, we are thrust into a dangerous world. For who decides what "good" is? It is sobering to think that the greatest sins committed by humankind – the starving to death of thirty million people in China during the Cultural Revolution and the murder of six million Jews by the Nazis – were legal according to the laws of the land in which each of these atrocities occurred.

Tolerance is a warm and cuddly word. But we shouldn't allow it to be a blanket under which we hide to avoid truth.

All good people want to be tolerant. Of course we should be civil towards others who think differently to us, but this shouldn't mean we dispense with the idea of truth. We must be allowed to search, explore, and disagree. The important thing is not to be disagreeable in the process.

To tolerate everything is to believe that there are no universal truths, just personal convictions that may change according to the circumstances. Holding such a low view of truth is a very bleak position to adopt philosophically. It must inevitably result in pragmatic self-interest that competes against the interests of others.

This book invites you to take an exciting journey, to unfreeze old patterns of thinking, to consider the real significance of who you are, and to explore what your meaning is. Amidst the competing claims of a thousand different philosophies and religions, it dares to introduce you to the possibility of God – and for good reason.

Character and courage

Let me read to you a small excerpt from Lewis Carroll's *Alice in Wonderland*. Are you sitting comfortably? Then I shall begin:

> *"Cheshire Puss,"* she began, rather timidly, *"would you tell me, please, which way I ought to go from here?"*
>
> *"That depends a good deal on where you want to get to,"* said the cat.
>
> *"I don't much care where,"* said Alice.
>
> *"Then it doesn't matter which way you go,"* said the cat.

This little exchange prompts the question: Where do you want to go in life? I'm not talking about achieving goals such as paying off the mortgage or buying a new car. I'm asking what you want your life to count for.

If you believe life has meaning, then it is terribly important for you to discover what that meaning is and live in a way that reflects it. If you don't do this, you risk your life becoming shallow and self-obsessed.

A book by C.S. Lewis, *The Abolition of Man*, contains a chapter entitled "Men Without Chests". It is based on Plato's notion that the chest is the location of a person's spirit, heart, and character.[1] When contemporary culture gets locked into the idea of "doing your own thing" and denies any universal truth or value, it develops a mind that is adrift, not controlled by anything other than unbridled desires. The Bible speaks about people who think like this, saying, *"Their destiny is destruction, their god is their stomach, and their glory is in their shame. Their mind is set on earthly things"* (Philippians 3:19). Such people have no character, no chest.

There is another reason why it's important to find your true identity and meaning: quite simply, no one who lacks this knowledge is getting on very well. The famous psychologist and philosopher, Carl Jung, once wrote:

*About a third of my cases are suffering from no
clinically definable neurosis, but from the senselessness
and emptiness of their lives. This can be described as
the general neurosis of our time.*[2]

He was saying that there are an awful lot of people for whom life
seems utterly meaningless. They lack purpose.

But to find your purpose, you need to work at finding out
what is true.

Explore the possibility

The American journalist and satirist Henry Louis Mencken
(1888–1956) wrote:

*God is the immemorial refuge of the incompetent, the
helpless, the miserable. They find not only sanctuary in
his arms, but also a kind of superiority, soothing to their
macerated egos; he will set them above their betters.*[3]

Mencken is calling me incompetent, helpless, and miserable
because I'm a Christian. Fortunately, I know enough wonderful
and brilliant Christian people to convince me that he is quite
wrong.

There is good evidence that Christianity is more than a crutch
for ineffectual people with an anxiety complex. Christian faith is
historically, morally, and scientifically reasonable – and is held to
be true by millions of people across many nations and centuries.
While that doesn't prove anything, it should at least suggest that
we ought not to dismiss Christianity carelessly.

The fact that anything bothers to exist at all demands more
from us than a shrug of the shoulders. To believe the universe

came from nothing, and that its incredible mathematical order is meaningless, takes very great faith. It is not a faith I share. Neither is it one shared by thousands of the world's most eminent scientists.

So, while our physical existence doesn't prove God's existence, it does challenge us to think about the possibility of God.

The subtlety of God

If Christianity is right, then God is not one to prove his existence with overwhelming displays of might. God is subtle. He invites rather than coerces. Throughout this book, you will hear this refrain repeated time and again in different contexts. God whispers his invitation in the cosmos and in nature. His voice is insistent. It is always gentle, yet it can be heard by anyone. As such, you will not find a "knockout" proof of God in any of these chapters. There is simply a whisper of God that is intellectually reasonable.

If God exists, then all truth (both scientific and theological) comes from the essence of who he is. This means, logically, that it is perfectly reasonable for science to point to the possibility of God. Certainly, science cannot get in the way of anyone coming to God.

The genius of God, however, is that he cannot be known through intellectual study alone, for that would mean Christianity is reserved for academic elites. The only way to know God is through the humbling door of faith. Faith is the great leveller. The professor, the peasant, the child with Down's syndrome, the Olympic star, and the prime minister all need faith. This is why Jesus taught that unless we have faith as humble and trusting as that of a little child, we will not enter the kingdom of God (Mark 10:15). God never compromises on the need for faith.

This doesn't mean there is no place for reason. Science and reason can (and should) point to the possibility of God – as I hope this book will show. Both can lead you to the doorway to God, but neither can force you through it. To go in, you will need to take a step of faith – faith that is informed by reason.

If you look at the door between yourself and God, you will see that it is very low. You must bend low with humility to go through. If you take another look at the door, you will notice that Jesus has unlocked it and is there ready to meet you. He stands waiting to take you on from where science has left you. But only you can decide whether or not to walk through.

Dare to think big

This book invites you to be thoroughly discontent with shallow thinking. It is an invitation to think about the big questions of life, to discover who you are and why you exist. These are vital issues. So, may I encourage you to think big? Dare to read God's signature on the invitations he's sent you. Learn to be amazed at the things around you. Let yourself say "Wow!" frequently.

More than a "nasty smell"

If there is no God to give meaning and worth, then we are simply an organic accident that has drifted aimlessly to the top of an evolutionary tree to flourish briefly before dying and leaving a rather nasty smell.

My hope is that when you die, you will leave more than a "nasty smell".

Enjoy the adventure of this book.

I

THE EVIDENCE OF GOD IN THE COSMOS

The universe is amazing – I mean, really, really amazing. It blows your mind.

And I have a sneaking suspicion that it is meant to. Certainly, the modernist dictum that "a scientific breakthrough a day will keep the need for God away" has started to look a little dog-eared in recent decades. The more scientists understand the universe, the more mysterious and spectacular it becomes.

This fact is not always appreciated.

I once listened to a symphony orchestra play Rachmaninoff's Symphony No 2. Now, Rach was a bloke who knew how to use an orchestra. Big, rich tones poured out like a well-aged Shiraz. This was no sweet, demure work content to be played in the background. It demanded your attention and mugged your emotions. From my vantage point in the balcony, I glanced down on the people below… and was staggered to see someone engrossed in their smart-phone.

It seems that no matter what amazing spectacle you place in front of people, some will choose not to see it.

So, let's agree to give ourselves permission to wonder and be amazed, to recover the childlike delight of saying "Wow!" – because I think we are meant to. I think God hangs his business card in the cosmos and invites us to see it. A 3,000-year-old songwriter certainly seemed to think so. The psalmist writes in the Old Testament:

The heavens declare the glory of God; the skies
proclaim the work of his hands. Day after day they
pour forth speech; night after night they reveal
knowledge. They have no speech, they use no words; no
sound is heard from them. Yet their voice goes out into
all the earth, their words to the ends of the world.

(Psalm 19:1–4)

I believe it is reasonable to suggest that the outrageous bigness and splendour of the cosmos is an invitation for us to consider the possibility of a Creator and perhaps learn a few things about him. Doing so should ensure that any conclusions we draw about God are in harmony with the best understandings we have of science.

It's worth noting, in passing, that the Apostle Paul believed it was reasonable to expect people to ponder the significance of creation and to let this introduce them to the possibility of God. In fact, they were culpable if they did not:

For since the creation of the world God's invisible
qualities – his eternal power and divine nature – have
been clearly seen, being understood from what has
been made, so that people are without excuse.

(Romans 1:20)

Now, that's a bold statement!

Aren't scientific truths and theological truths irreconcilable?

No.

Perhaps I should explain. If God exists, then all truth has its origin in God – including scientific truth and theological truth. Because the two truths both derive from the essence of who God is, the two disciplines cannot fight each other. They might answer different questions, but they must ultimately be compatible. Indeed, it would be reasonable to expect each discipline to give a deeper perspective of the other. Theology goes deeper than the "how" and "when" of science, and asks why things are as they are. It seeks to do more than say, "Things exist simply because they do." Theology, therefore, puts science in a bigger context. This brings to mind Einstein's famous aphorism, "*Science without religion is lame; religion without science is blind.*"[1]

It's worth pausing here to talk a little about Einstein. If you do an Internet search for "Einstein and Christianity" you will discover an unseemly squabble between Christians wanting to claim Einstein was a Christian, and atheists who want to insist he was an atheist. Each wants Einstein, and his genius, to be on their side to lend them credibility.

The truth is actually much more interesting – and, I submit, significant.

Einstein was a brilliant scientist. He was not, however, a brilliant theologian. It is perhaps unfair of people to expect him to be one: theology was not his area of study. What is highly significant is that science took Einstein as far as it could towards God. Einstein's scientific study convinced him of the existence of God. Like the philosopher Spinoza, he believed the universe and the physical laws of nature to be expressions of God. As such, science gave good reason to believe in a higher being. However, that was as far as he was able to go. Although he was firmly convinced of the historical reality of Jesus Christ, he was not a Christian. He didn't believe in a personal God who had a plan for humankind. Rather, Einstein believed that humanity existed solely because of the cause and effect of physical laws – a view that has more in common with deism.

The fact that Einstein had this understanding is perhaps not surprising. Einstein's parents were atheistic Jews, so he didn't have a Christian heritage. He'd also experienced some overbearing behaviour from church institutions and this did nothing to endear him to conventional Christianity. Consequently, Einstein contented himself with being a theist. Why? Because that's where science took him. For him to know a personal God, he would have needed to journey on from science – into a knowledge of Jesus Christ. He did not make that journey.

The significance of Einstein's story is that science led one of the greatest minds of modern history to God. To suggest that science must inevitably do the opposite is therefore quite wrong.

The universe is very big and very mysterious

The first thing the cosmos suggests about God is that he has a majesty beyond that which our minds can comprehend. The night sky has amazed people from the Bronze Age to the age of the Higgs boson.

Here are some basic statistics.

We live on the third planet out from a middle-aged star called the Sun. That star sits three-quarters of the way along the edge of one of the spiral arms of a galaxy called the Milky Way, containing about 300 billion stars. If that wasn't extraordinary enough, our home galaxy of 300 billion stars is just one of over 100 billion galaxies in the universe. And this mind-bogglingly huge universe exploded into being from a tiny, almost infinitely dense particle (called a "singularity") about 13.7 billion years ago.

You can't help but get the feeling that God might have been showing off, just a bit.

The universe is certainly big. We have to measure the distances between galaxies and stars using the speed of light. As light scurries on at the goodly pace of nearly 300,000 kilometres per second, you can imagine it would cover a fair distance at that speed over a whole year. We call this distance a "light-year", and that's what astronomers use to measure the distance between stars and galaxies.

The nearest star to our Sun (Proxima Centauri) is a paltry 4.3 light-years away. This compares favourably with the distance to our nearest neighbouring galaxy, which is 163,000 light-years away. All this, and you haven't yet begun to seriously journey across the universe. Oh, I forgot to mention: the universe is expanding at an ever-increasing rate, so it's getting bigger all the time!

The universe is not only big, it is mysterious. In fact, only 5 per cent of it is visible, with 27 per cent of it thought to be composed of "dark matter", and 68 per cent thought to be composed of "dark energy". Dark matter neither absorbs nor emits any form of electromagnetic radiation, so it can't be seen. We only know it's there because of the gravitational effect it has on other heavenly bodies.

Dark energy is something of a hypothesis only. Scientists have very little idea of what it is, but they think that it is the energy that is causing the universe to expand at an ever-accelerating rate. Certainly, some sort of force is doing this and overcoming the natural tendency for gravity to cause the heavenly bodies to crunch back together again.

You're a star

Let's talk about stars. Our Sun has a diameter about 109 times greater than the Earth. That's pretty impressive. Now imagine a star that is 1,500 times bigger than the Sun. That's the size of the red supergiant NML Cygni. To put that into perspective, if you placed Cygni at the centre of our solar system, its surface would extend beyond the orbit of Jupiter and half way to Saturn. That's big!

Stars are a crucial part of our universe – and the mechanism by which they are made is fascinating. They are made on tendrils of cosmic dust. These are known as elephant trunks and they poke out of giant dust clouds. The elephant trunks are often a light-year long, so they're pretty big. Blobs of dust float off them into space. Gravity then causes the dust in these blobs to clump together, and to do so with such force that hydrogen is fused into helium, producing a massive release of heat. When that happens, hey presto! You have a star. Gravity keeps pressing in, causing this reaction to continue over billions of years.

This amazing scenario has given enough time to allow life to evolve on the third planet out from a middle-aged star – planet Earth.

Stars like our Sun are, in fact, giant ovens that cook up hydrogen and helium to form all the atoms in the periodic table up to the weight of iron. Heavier elements can only be made by the exceedingly high temperatures and pressures that occur when very big stars die in supernova explosions. All dying stars then scatter their atoms into the cosmos. Some of these atoms then clump together to form planets such as our Earth.

It's worth pondering a moment what this means. Look at yourself in a mirror. Every atom that exists within you was once cooked up inside a star. You are made of star stuff! You truly are a walking cosmic drama.

The fact that the universe is capable of producing stars stable enough to burn long enough to allow life to develop is consistent with the principles taught in the first book of the Bible, Genesis. The biblical creation accounts make it clear that because a rational God has caused the universe to exist, it is a rational, stable place. You may not be impressed by this, but it is actually very different to most of the thinking that was around in ancient times.

The Genesis account of Noah's ark and the flood has some similarities with the ancient Mesopotamian epic of Gilgamesh. In fact, it's quite possible that the early biblical authors felt free to borrow its framework in order to write God's story. But in doing so, they made an important distinction. Whereas the ancient Mesopotamians were terrified that the world would collapse into chaos at any moment, the writers of Genesis wanted us to understand that God's creation was stable and presided over by a benevolent God.

This matches what we see. The fact that the universe appears ordered and operates according to beautiful mathematical equations suggests the existence of a mind. While our universe is one in which suffering and extinctions occur, this should not blind us to the fact that it is amazingly well ordered and appears to be finely tuned in order to allow life. Scientific observation therefore supports the teaching of Genesis, which says there is a mind behind the order of the universe.

Multiverses and turtles

An objection to this thinking has come from those who believe our universe is just one of an infinite number of universes – which, because there are an infinite number of them, must eventually chance upon a set of scientific rules able to develop intelligent life. After all, if this were not so, we wouldn't be here to observe ourselves.

We'll talk more about "multiverses" later, but the challenge to the existence of God posed by multiverses can be met in part by saying this: It isn't just *that* we exist which is the miracle; it is the *manner* of our existence. The self-observing life form we call "humanity" is not simply a blob of brain able to know itself to be alive for a brief moment of time. It is significantly more. It is Mozart. It is Mother Teresa. It is humour, compassion, creativity, love, heroism, and science. It is also a shy but persistent ache that compels 96 per cent of us to reach towards a higher being, someone who will give us meaning. The life form that is us really is very remarkable – too remarkable, I suggest, to lazily dismiss as simply the chance product of an infinite number of universes.

So, it is not just a case of life existing but of appreciating the *manner* and *nature* of that life.

I've heard someone explain the significance of this with an analogy.

Suppose some drug smugglers had tampered with your travelling case while you were touring in a foreign country, and customs officials had found five kilograms of heroin inside it. The judge refuses to believe you are innocent and condemns you to be shot to death by a firing squad. You are led out of prison, placed against a wall, and blindfolded. Ten of the army's top marksmen stand eight paces away. At a command from the officer, they cock their weapons. Then you hear, "Ready, aim… FIRE!"

To your amazement, you discover that you are still alive. You feel all over your body, but don't find any bullet holes. Might I suggest that at this point you would do more than shrug with indifference and say, "Well, since I'm here to report on the situation, I must have chanced upon a set of circumstances that has enabled me to do so." No. You would justifiably seek some sort of explanation.

Caution needs to be exercised when using the term "infinite" to dilute the significance of the existence of humankind. The word "infinite" is not an escape clause that allows any possibility. It is not a magician's hat from which anything can be produced. We still need to ask: Who or what began the first universe? Why has "chance" been given the opportunity to build a universe that is able to develop humankind?

You do not explain a book simply by pointing to a library of books. Neither do you explain our ordered universe by pointing to the possibility of an infinite number of universes. More needs to be said.

On the first page of his book *A Brief History of Time* Stephen Hawking describes a conversation in which a woman disagrees with a scientist's description of the solar system. She says something like this: "You are quite wrong, young man. The world is really a giant plate sitting on the back of a giant turtle."

"And what's the turtle sitting on?" replies the scientist.

"Young man, you can't trick me. It's standing on another turtle. There are turtles all the way down."[2]

While we might smile at the naivety of the woman, all that atheistic scientists are proposing with their multitude of universes… is a multitude of turtles. They don't actually answer the question.

The cosmologist Paul Davies agrees:

> *The multiverse theory is increasingly popular, but it doesn't so much explain the laws of physics as dodge the whole issue. There has to be a physical mechanism to make all those universes and bestow bylaws on them. This process will require its own laws, or meta-laws. Where do they come from? The problem has*

26

simply been shifted up a level from the laws of the
universe to the meta-laws of the multiverse.[3]

Who's monkeyed with the physics?

Many of the world's top scientists who claim no faith are scornful of those who suggest that the evolution of intelligent life in the cosmos is purely the product of chance. This, I suggest, is significant.

One of them was the English physicist and astronomer Fred Hoyle (1915–2001). Notwithstanding his atheistic convictions, Hoyle wrote that the likelihood of chance alone being responsible for making even the simplest of living cells was about the same as that of a tornado sweeping through a junkyard and assembling a Boeing 747 aeroplane.[4]

Hoyle's atheistic convictions were shaken a number of times in his life. It happened when he was trying to work out how a carbon atom could be made. As all living things are carbon-based, it was a relevant question. The trouble was, it seemed that making carbon inside a star from the component atoms of beryllium and helium was impossible. The necessary intermediate reaction states were just too unstable to allow time for a carbon atom to be made. Fred therefore reasoned that there had to be a special "resonance state" within the nucleus of carbon that would allow reaction rates to increase dramatically, and that this energy state would need to correlate exactly to the temperature found inside a star. He managed to persuade a research team at California Institute of Technology to look for this proposed resonance state. They found it at the temperature Hoyle predicted. When they did, Hoyle wrote:

A common sense interpretation of the facts suggests
that a superintellect has monkeyed with physics, as

well as with chemistry and biology, and that there are
no blind forces worth speaking about in nature.[5]

Coincidences like this have even caused the physicist Stephen Hawking, who is ambivalent and sometimes antagonistic about faith, to wonder about religious implications. He once said, *"The odds against a universe like ours emerging out of something like the Big Bang are enormous. I think there are clearly religious implications."*[6]

I think he's right.

The anthropic principle

The fact that our universe seems remarkably conducive to the evolution of intelligent life has led to the development of the "anthropic principle". This is the idea that the universe appears to exist in a very precise way which has allowed the existence of humankind. (Anthropic literally means "of humankind".)

Certainly, our universe is very special. Billions of things had to be just right for life as we know it to evolve. This is particularly the case for the four main forces foundational for the existence of our universe. These forces are (1) gravity, (2) the electromagnetic force, (3) the "strong" nuclear force, and (4) the "weak" nuclear force. The strength of these forces was established less than a millionth of a second after the Big Bang. Now here's the thing: If the value of any one of these forces had differed even slightly, the universe could not exist. For instance, if the ratio between the strong nuclear force and the electromagnetic force had differed by one part in 100,000,000,000,000,000, no stars could have formed.

Similarly, the force of the Big Bang had to be just right. The universe could not expand too quickly or it would become too diluted for matter to clump together to form galaxies. However, it could not expand too slowly, or gravity would cause it to clump back together too quickly to allow time for life to develop.

The universe also needed to have matter scattered evenly throughout it, otherwise there would be catastrophic cosmic turbulence. But the distribution of matter could not be too even; it had to exist in clumps so that galaxies could form.

We even needed to have the right planetary neighbours. Without a massive planet like Jupiter nearby to drag asteroids away from us with its gravity, a thousand times as many would hit the Earth's surface – and life could not exist.

The level of fine-tuning necessary to allow life to exist defies imagination. I would like to suggest that God's signature is writ large on the cosmos… and that it is there for those who want to take notice of it.

Copernicus and Galileo… and their fracas with the church

No discussion about God, Christianity, and the universe would be complete without talking about Copernicus and Galileo. Atheists often cite the rather shabby behaviour of the church towards these two astronomers in the sixteenth and seventeenth centuries as proof that Christianity is inherently antagonistic towards science.

In reality, the relationship of these two men with the church was a great deal more complex than those pushing ideological barrows would have us believe. Let me explain.

The Polish astronomer Nicolaus Copernicus (1473–1543) popularized the idea that the Earth rotated on its axis once daily and travelled around the Sun once annually.

Copernicus sent his ideas around to respected astronomers in 1513. This work gave him such standing in society that he was invited, the following year, by the Roman Catholic Church to resolve the problem of their yearly calendar, which had become inaccurate by an extraordinary ten days!

Some years later (in 1533), Pope Clement VII and some cardinals heard a presentation of Copernicus's theory about the movement of the Earth given by his papal secretary, John Widmanstad, in the Vatican Gardens. It is worth noting that no antagonism was expressed in response to this presentation. In fact, Cardinal Schönberg wrote a kindly letter to Copernicus (via the hand of John Widmanstad) a few years later. This is what he said:

> *Nicholas Schönberg, Cardinal of Capua,*
> *to Nicholas Copernicus,*
>
> *Greetings.*
>
> *Some years ago, word reached me concerning your*
> *proficiency, of which everybody constantly spoke.*
> *At that time I began to have a very high regard for*
> *you, and also to congratulate our contemporaries*
> *among whom you enjoyed such great prestige. For I*
> *had learned that you had not merely mastered the*
> *discoveries of the ancient astronomers uncommonly*
> *well but had also formulated a new cosmology.*
>
> *In it you maintain that the Earth moves; that the*
> *sun occupies the lowest, and thus the central, place in*
> *the universe; that the eighth heaven remains perpetually*
> *motionless and fixed; and that, together with the*
> *elements included in its sphere, the moon, situated*
> *between the heavens of Mars and Venus, revolves*

around the sun in the period of a year.

I have also learned that you have written an exposition of this whole system of astronomy, and have computed the planetary motions and set them down in tables, to the greatest admiration of all. Therefore with the utmost earnestness I entreat you, most learned sir, unless I inconvenience you, to communicate this discovery of yours to scholars, and at the earliest possible moment to send me your writings on the sphere of the universe together with the tables and whatever else you may have that is relevant to this subject.

Moreover, I have instructed Theodoric of Reden to have everything copied in your quarters at my expense and dispatched to me. If you gratify my desire in this matter, you will see that you are dealing with a man who is zealous for your reputation and eager to do justice to so fine a talent.

Farewell.

Rome, 1 November 1536.

Copernicus was so encouraged by this letter that he included it as the introduction to his famous book, *De Revolutionibus Orbium Coelestium*. This book had a foreword written by the Lutheran theologian Andreas Osiander, and the entire work was dedicated to Pope Paul III. With the encouragement of Tiedeman Giese, the Bishop of Kulm, Copernicus's book was published in 1543, just months after his death. It was said that he held a copy of the book in his hands just before he died.

At this point, there was no hint of ecclesiastical censure.

De Revolutionibus did not become contentious until Aristotelian philosophers began objecting to it. They said it challenged the literal meaning of some texts in the Bible, particularly Joshua 10:12 where Joshua commanded the Sun to stand still so that he would have time to defeat the Amorites. The Aristotelian philosophers believed the Earth was a place of change and decay, whereas the heavens were perfect and unchangeable. For Copernicus to suggest that the Earth circled the Sun was a direct challenge to this view.

About this time, the Roman Catholic Church convened the Council of Trent in order to reform a church threatened by schism and which had been fractured by the Protestant Reformation. It was a lengthy affair that lasted from 1545 to 1563. One of the things the Council resolved was that only doctors of the Catholic Church were authorized to interpret Scripture. (The Protestants had made interpretation of Scripture a divisive affair.)

The Aristotelians used the church's disciplinary authority to attack not only Copernicus's ideas but also a new person who was now championing them: a scientist from Pisa by the name of Galileo Galilei. Galileo had developed the telescope and used it to make observations that supported Copernicus's theory.

Although Galileo had once enjoyed the favour of the Pope, he fell from grace for three reasons. First, the Aristotelians pointed out that Galileo was effectively reinterpreting Scripture without authority.

Second, Galileo did not have the "knock out" proof that he required to be totally convincing. He needed an instrument that was accurate enough to measure the angle to a distant star so that he could compare the star's position in winter with its position in summer. Aristotle himself had said centuries earlier that this was the proof that would be required to indicate that the Earth revolved around the Sun. The instrument capable of measuring this didn't exist until Joseph Fraunhofer built a heliometer some 200 years later. Friedrich Bessel was the first to use it to confirm the heliocentric movement of the Earth.

Third, Galileo sabotaged himself by doing some very unwise things. One of these was to put the Pope's arguments against Galileo's theory in the mouth of the fool Simplicius, a fictitious character in his book *Dialogue Concerning the Two Chief World Systems – Ptolemaic and Copernican*. This was published in 1632. The Pope had earlier given permission for Galileo to write a book presenting arguments for and against the Copernican theory, asking only that Galileo not merely advocate Copernicus's heliocentric view. It was a request that Galileo chose not to heed.

One way or another, things came to a head. Galileo was brought to trial on 22 June 1633, after which he was required under threat of torture to "abjure, curse and detest" his Copernican theories.

It is worth remembering that although Copernicus and Galileo fell foul of the Roman Catholic Church, both remained deeply religious men who were committed to their faith.

Some atheists have been guilty of recasting these events in order to paint the Christian church as "anti-science". This is a simplistic interpretation. Copernicus and Galileo actually fell foul of the politics of Aristotelian philosophers in a time of heightened sensitivities caused by the Reformation. Galileo also sabotaged his cause by his singular lack of tact.

One fiction sometimes heard is that Catholic clerics refused to look through Galileo's telescope. This was not so. It was the Aristotelian professors Cesare Cremonini and Giulio Libri who refused to look through it. In contrast, the Jesuit cardinal Bellarmine agreed to do so in 1611 (after first asking Jesuit scientists in the Vatican Observatory to verify that Galileo's telescope was observing true images and not simply flaws in the glass lens). The Jesuits were actually much taken with the telescope. One of them, Christoph Scheiner, used a telescope to record information about sunspots that he published a year later in 1612.

An indication of just how important it is to have a right understanding of what really happened between Copernicus, Galileo, and the church is shown by the fact that two nineteenth-century Americans – the educationalist and diplomat Andrew White, and the philosopher and physician John Draper – used the Galileo trial to help promote the notion that Christianity has always been at war with science. This is still believed by some today, even though serious scholarship has debunked the myth. (The erroneous idea that there is a war between science and Christianity will be explored further in the next chapter.)

It is good to know the facts. Truth is every bit as important in history as it is in science.

Please take care with your claims

It is worth us all retaining a degree of humility when searching for truth. Certainly, the scientific community needs to avoid the overbearing, all-controlling stance it once accused the Christian church of adopting at the start of the Enlightenment.

I say this because it is not always easy to separate fact from opinion in the writings of some of today's scientists. Stephen Gould's comment that humankind is no more than "*a fortuitous twig, budding but yesterday on an ancient and copious bush of (evolution)*"[7] is a personal conviction. It is not a scientific fact, for it belies the reasoning of other scientists such as the physicist and cosmologist Paul Davies, who says he belongs "*to the group of scientists who do not subscribe to a conventional religion but nevertheless deny that the universe is a purposeless accident. Through my scientific work I have come to believe more and more strongly that the universe is put together with an ingenuity so astonishing that I cannot accept it merely as a brute fact... I cannot believe that our existence in this universe is a mere quirk of fate, an accident of history, an incidental blip in the great cosmic drama. Our involvement is too intimate... We are truly meant to be here."[8]*

Ideological blinkers exist in the scientific community just as much as anywhere else. Steven Weinberg concludes his book, *The First Three Minutes*, by saying that it is farcical to think that human beings are anything more than an "*outcome of a chain of accidents reaching back to the first three minutes... [Earth] is just a tiny part of an overwhelmingly hostile universe... The more the universe seems comprehensible, the more it also seems pointless.*"[9]

In contrast to this, Freeman Dyson, a research physicist at the Advanced Institute at Princeton, looks at the same cosmos and says, "*The more I examine the universe and study details of its architecture, the more evidence I find that the universe in some sense must have known that we were coming.*"[10] This leads Dyson to say, "*Twentieth Century science provides a solid foundation for a philosophy of hope.*"[11]

So, scientists: don't lock yourself into an empiricist prison that fails to allow for the possibility of God. You don't have the evidence to do so. Humility and honesty are required. And do be careful with your claims. Non-scientists may not have the skill to determine when you are straying from empirical fact to philosophical speculation.

Motives that are not so pure

One of the few good things to come out of postmodern thinking about science is the realization that science is rarely conducted objectively and with pure motives. All scientists bring baggage (ideologies and preconceptions) to their scientific enquiry. While this should not affect the manner of their scientific enquiry (the process for authentic scientific enquiry is well established), it can affect what is studied, why it is studied, the application of what is studied, and the significance ascribed to the study. As such, science is not as pure as some rational empiricists would claim. The humanity of scientific researchers stubbornly emerges like weeds in a vegetable patch.

Let me give you some examples.

Despite compelling evidence for the universe beginning with a Big Bang (evidence obtained by satellites measuring the temperature of space and photographing the ripples in the background radiation of space), the English physicist Fred Hoyle didn't want to believe it. He wanted to believe in a "steady state" eternal universe that had always existed. His unwillingness to believe in the Big Bang had nothing to do with any scientific objection. He objected to the concept simply because he was an atheist. He didn't want to consider anything so inexplicable as a beginning because it suggested that God would be necessary to push the start button. (The difficulty in explaining the ultimate origin of why things exist without factoring in God is shown by Terry Pratchett's whimsical comment: "*In the beginning there was nothing, which exploded.*"[12])

The concept of the Big Bang was also viewed with suspicion by Soviet cosmologists during the Cold War. The American scientific historian Loren Graham mentions a book by V.I. Sviderskii, published in 1956, which rejected the Big Bang model and described it as an "*unscientific Popish conclusion*".[13] This, I submit, is not a scientific comment.

Even the search for a theory that might allow for the existence of an infinite number of universes (so nullifying the significance of our own universe) is not without grubby ideological fingerprints. The Russian American theoretical physicist Andrei Linde admitted that his work on inflation theory and the concept of multiverses was partly motivated by his ideological difficulties with questions like, "Who gave the command for the universe?"[14]

Recent ripples

Whenever there is a significant cosmic discovery, TV chat show hosts invariably put forward the proposition that our new understanding has made the idea of God obsolete. It happened with the discovery of the ripples in the background radiation left over from the Big Bang, and it happened again when a telescope at the Amundsen–Scott South Pole Station collected data between January 2010 and December 2012 for "The Background Imaging of Cosmic Extragalactic Polarization 2" (BICEP2) experiment. Just over two years later, the results were published. There was huge excitement because the researchers claimed to have found ripples in the universe called gravitational waves. These ripples were first mooted to exist by the American physicist Alan Guth, of the Massachusetts Institute of Technology, when he proposed the theory of "inflation" in 1980. This theory proposed that the universe expanded faster than the speed of light in the first fraction of a nanosecond after it was born. If this was the case, scientists felt that such an event would have caused ripples in the fabric of "space-time".

Scientists claimed to have identified these ripples in 2014. Other scientists, however, have since challenged their findings, saying that the readings could have come from dust clouds within our own galaxy.

If these ripples have, in fact, been found, they would, of course, neither prove nor disprove God. They would simply help us to understand the mechanism whereby a remarkable and highly unlikely universe came into existence. The "why" behind the "how" still requires explanation.

Both science and Christianity require faith

It is not the case that science is driven by scepticism, observation, and experiment, while Christianity requires you to believe ten impossible things before breakfast. Science and Christianity are both built on evidence... and both require faith.

Paul Davies puts this well. He says:

All science proceeds on the assumption that nature is ordered in a rational and intelligible way. You couldn't be a scientist if you thought the universe was a meaningless jumble of odds and ends haphazardly juxtaposed. When physicists probe to a deeper level of subatomic structure, or astronomers extend the reach of their instruments, they expect to encounter additional elegant mathematical order.[15]

He goes on to say that the intelligibility of the cosmos is reflected in the laws of physics – the fundamental rules that determine how nature runs. These laws of physics are regarded as sacrosanct, as phenomena that have always existed in our universe. The obvious question prompted by this is, of course, "Where did these laws come from?" After all, the idea that they exist without reason is anti-rational. This is not a question that can be shrugged aside.

Davies says, *"Clearly, then, both religion and science are founded on faith – namely, on belief in the existence of something outside the universe, like an unexplained God or an unexplained set of physical laws."*

He concludes by saying, *"Until science comes up with a testable theory of the laws of the universe, its claim to be free of faith is manifestly bogus."*[16]

That's not a bad conclusion from a renowned scientist with no conventional faith.

A tree in the desert

Those who point to the size of the cosmos in order to dismiss the significance of Earth have an invalid argument. If you take a beautiful, blue planet that has intelligent life on it and put it alongside a hundred other planets that don't have life, it doesn't make the blue planet any less remarkable. If you put the same blue planet against a million or a billion other planets that don't have life, that doesn't make it any less remarkable either. Until it can be shown that the universe is teeming with intelligent life that has come about as the result of common chemical processes, life on Earth has every right to consider itself to be pretty special.

I once buried a small golden bead in a large tray of sand, then invited the members of a youth group to find it by digging through the sand with tablespoons and pouring what they scooped through a sieve to see if they had unearthed it. No one did. When I retrieved the gold bead, I asked them if it was any less significant simply because it was surrounded by lots of very common sand.

They all answered "No".

I then suggested that in the same way, our Earth remains special, even though it is surrounded by a very large universe.

The physicist Robert Russell makes the same point using the analogy of a tree in a desert. He says:

> *Suppose you are lost and thirsty in a vast, dry desert. Suddenly you spot a palm tree on the horizon. Are you going to say, "Well since the desert is so vast and barren, that wavy tree is insignificant, a statistical fluke not worth taking seriously"?*[17]

Please don't lightly dismiss the uniqueness of your own planet.

And to help you remember this, here's a quip by the Scottish comedian Arnold Brown: "*I sometimes look at the stars and think: how significant I am.*"

Good night, it's all over: making sense of the end of the universe

I like happy endings… but the prospect that our universe has one is remote.

Scientists tell us that our Sun will die in 4.5 billion years' time. Sadly, if you manage to escape to another solar system on a spacecraft, you are not out of the woods, because the universe itself is due to die and fade away into low-level radiation – an event which scientists have dubbed "heat death".

The astrophysicist and theologian David Wilkinson writes, "*This end of Universe in the heat death of futility raises a great deal of pessimism within the scientific community.*"[18] Paul Davies is one who typifies this feeling. He says: "*[An] almost empty universe growing steadily more cold and dark for all eternity is profoundly depressing.*"[19]

Atheistic philosophers are no happier. The twentieth-century English philosopher Bertrand Russell wrote:

> *The world which science presents for our belief is even more purposeless, and more void of meaning... all the labours of the ages, all the devotion, all the inspiration, all the noonday brightness of human genius, are destined to extinction... and the whole temple of man's achievements must inevitably be buried beneath the debris of a universe in ruins.*[20]

The huge question each of us needs to answer is, "Why?" Why does anything exist at all? Does our existence have any meaning, particularly in the light of the fact that our universe will end?

Science is, and has to be, silent on this. For more understanding, we need to turn to theology.

Meeting some objections

Two objections are commonly aired when considering evidence for the proposition that God intended humanity to exist. So, let's take a look at them.

Objection 1: *Humans occupy such a minuscule part of the universe that it is impossible to believe we are in any way significant.*

The theoretical physicist John Polkinghorne does not agree. He says that we need not be upset about our apparent insignificance in a large universe. The universe had to be as big as it is, he reasoned, if life was to develop on any one planet. The size of the universe was necessary so that planets and galaxies were far enough apart to avoid gravity clumping them back together before intelligent life could evolve.[21]

Can I be honest and confess to some mild frustration at being caught between two groups of atheists saying different things? One group seems unable to appreciate the bigness and wonder of the cosmos, and therefore fails to see any evidence of divine mind. The other sees the vastness of the universe very clearly, and concludes that we are so insignificant that we could not possibly be intended by a god.

I'd like to get the two groups together!

Let's leave the last word on this to C.S. Lewis, who said, "*If it is maintained that anything so small as the Earth must, in any event, be too unimportant to merit the love of the Creator, we reply that no Christian ever supposed we did merit it.*"[22]

Objection 2: *It is probable that the universe is teeming with other forms of intelligent life, which, if true, makes a nonsense of the special status of humankind.*

While precursors to life on Earth may have been splashed onto Earth by meteorites crashing into Mars, there is, as yet, no evidence of any intelligent life existing elsewhere in the universe. It would be unwise to allow mere speculation to cancel out the wonder of what unquestionably does exist.

If intelligent life were found elsewhere in the universe, this need not necessarily be incompatible with Christianity. It might indicate that life is not due to unlikely chance events but to the guiding hand of God who has designed an inherently fruitful universe.

Jesus makes sense of it

If we concede that there is good reason to believe God exists, what can we know about him?

Is God just an impersonal force that puts the ingredients of a self-developing universe together, then steps back behind the veil of mystery to watch what galaxies, planets and life forms will come into existence? Is God's role simply to invent and sustain a giant game of chance? Did God specifically intend humankind or not? Are we the chance winners of an evolutionary race, destined to flourish briefly until we are overtaken by other life forms on our planet?

If we were to rely on science alone, we might think this was the case. However, the event that crashes against such mournful thinking is God's self-revelation to us, most significantly as Jesus.

The fact that God has demonstrated his love for us through Jesus answers why the universe bothers to exist. It indicates that God is intentional and is the driving force behind the evolution of human beings. God's love for his creation transforms a chance existence into a divine goal, the meaningless into the sacred, the unplanned into the purposed, the impersonal into the personal, and the unloved into the cherished.

Hope

In the midst of our bewilderment about our existence, God reached down to humanity in Jesus, declared his love for us, showed us his character, died a hideous death to pay the price for our sins, and now invites us to share in the adventures of eternity with him. Another name for Jesus – *Immanuel* – literally means "God with us". God is with us, and that gives us hope.

All atheists can do is wave their fists in defiance at meaninglessness and strive to manufacture the illusion of progress to distract themselves from the fact that the only thing they have to look forward to is futility.

In contrast to this, Christians have an eternal hope. The Apostle Paul wrote, "*If only for this life we have hope in Christ, we are of all people most to be pitied*" (1 Corinthians 15:19). He expressed the idea again when writing to the Ephesians: "*Remember that at that time you were separate from Christ, excluded from citizenship in Israel and foreigners to the covenants of the promise, without hope and without God in the world*" (Ephesians 2:12).

It may interest you to know that in Hebrew, the word "hope", *tiqvah*, literally means "a twisted cord used to attach" (that is, to make safe). Without hope, therefore, you are unsafe.

How safe are you feeling?

Conclusion

As a scientist, I can tell you that the odds against you coming into existence were enormous. Our universe is very special. It is sometimes referred to as the "baby bear" universe (from the Goldilocks fairy tale) because it is "just right".

There are many things, it seems, which happen to be just right. The English physicist, Stephen Hawking, speaks about one of them, saying, "*If the rate of expansion one second after the big bang had been smaller by even one part in a hundred thousand million, million, the universe would have re-collapsed before it even reached its present size.*"[23]

They are odds you wouldn't like to bet on in a horse race!

So, I invite you to marvel at the fact that you exist – for when you understand how miraculous your existence is, a whole lot of truth about your significance on this planet will become evident.

It will invite you to consider the possibility that God intends you to exist, and that he has worked through the laws of nature to see that you do.

Now if this is true, then you are faced with a whole new set of realities:

- While you may not have been planned by your parents, you have been planned by God.

- Although there are 6.5 billion people on this planet, you matter.

- Your life is not yours to throw away. God has a plan for it.

- You have the right to inherit the purposes that God has reserved for you.

- You must honour other people who have also been intended by God.

You are meant to exist.

2

THE EVIDENCE OF GOD IN NATURE

This probably isn't very comforting, but you are a bit of an oddity. Your existence as a carbon-based life form is a highly unlikely thing. Just getting the carbon atom, as I said in the last chapter, was unlikely enough, but that's only the beginning of some rather amazing things that needed to happen in order to produce you.

One of the things that causes scientists to wonder is protein. You're made of quite a lot of it.

The idea of God making things took a bit of a battering in 1953 when Harold Urey and Stanley Millar, researchers at the University of Chicago, introduced some electrical sparks to a mixture of gasses and water that simulated the Earth's early atmosphere. After a few days, the water discoloured with a mixture of amino acids. As amino acids are the building blocks of protein, the basis of all life, some people claimed that the idea of God was redundant. Brute circumstances can bring about the existence of amino acids by chance. The mystery of how proteins and life came about was solved.

Alas, this was not so. Leaving aside the rather obvious fact that God began with nothing – no laboratory, no flasks, no chemicals, no physical laws – the fact is that while making amino acids is relatively easy, making proteins capable of sustaining life is mind-bogglingly difficult.

To build a protein, you have to put amino acids in precisely the right sequence. As a typical protein consists of 200 amino acids, the likelihood of making a protein molecule by chance would be equivalent to spinning a slot machine with 200 wheels, each with 20 symbols (to represent the 20 most common amino acids)... and then getting the winning combination.

You don't reckon that's a big deal? Let me explain. It would require you to spin the wheels more times than there are atoms in the universe.[1]

It has become almost a reflex action of the human psyche to explain the existence of highly unlikely complex structures by attributing them to evolution. The trouble is, no mechanism that allows the evolution of proteins has yet been discovered. This is not to say that it won't be discovered. But the fact that no mechanism has yet been discovered should at least mollify some atheistic hubris and lend it a blush of humility. The brutal reality is this: Evolution, as it is currently understood, can only work at the level of living organisms that are able to reproduce and die – and a complex protein molecule is not a living organism.

If the problem of building a protein wasn't big enough, there remains the rather obvious question of what it is exactly that brings life. What is the mysterious thing that enlivens trillions of uncaring atoms to build a living and breathing you?

It's odd seeing a dead body. I've seen a few as I've watched the strange phenomenon called "life" trickle away... turning a friend into a corpse. The really weird thing is that the body, at the point of death, contains all the elements necessary for life to exist – and yet there is only death. So, what is the mysterious life force that breathes fire into the unlikely pile of atoms that make up your body? And, more intriguingly, why does this life force exist? These musings bring to mind a comment by St Augustine:

And men go abroad to admire the heights of
mountains, the mighty waves of the sea, the broad tides
of rivers, the compass of the ocean, and the circuits
of the stars, yet pass over the mystery of themselves
without a thought.[2]

When pondering the possibility of God, it is important to study nature. If God exists, then the canvas upon which he painted his purposes was biology. The objects that God chooses to create and love are cast in the form of living, biological machines. As such, it is reasonable to expect that God might have left some clues to his own existence, character, and purposes in nature.

If the biblical witness to God is true, we would expect these clues to be subtle so that they don't compel faith in God, but invite it. The question, then, is, "Do we see evidence of God in nature?"

Please don't use God as a gap-filler

In ancient times, human beings were not as scientifically informed as they are today. They operated on the premise of "cause and effect". If something existed that was extraordinarily complex and ordered, experience had taught them that it was the product of mind. So, when they saw the complexity of nature, they ascribed it to a mind – a mind that they called "god". Sometimes, they ascribed it to many gods. They sought to understand and define those gods through their own cultural filters, a process that has resulted in the existence of more than 4,000 religions today.

On the face of it, this was pretty reasonable. Evidence suggested the existence of an intelligence behind the order of creation. Two things then occurred in human history to modify this understanding.

The first was the insertion of Jesus Christ into human history. No longer did humanity have to invent religions to try to reach God; God had come to us and was reaching out to us in Christ Jesus. The historical reality of Jesus, as witnessed to by contemporary historians (such as the Roman historian Tacitus and the uncontested parts of the writings of the Jewish historian Josephus), now informed our understanding of things.

The second was the emergence of the discipline of science, which people found to be remarkably fruitful in uncovering the causes of much that was previously mysterious and inexplicable. Many of these mysterious and inexplicable things had been attributed to the direct action of God. With advances in science, however, the complexity of a seashell and the path of a meteorite through the night sky were no longer explained as being the direct actions of a god. Consequently, the need to invoke God to explain things began to retreat.

This was not the killer blow to theistic faith that some atheists assert. Far from it. Evidence of reason and mind pervades the universe just as much today as at any other time in history. What it did mean was that God's involvement was a good deal more subtle; it indicated that he chooses to work through the laws of nature – laws that he put in place to build a universe.

God should not be lazily invoked to explain gaps in our scientific knowledge. This is because whenever something previously ascribed to God's action subsequently becomes explained by science, the need to postulate the existence of God retreats. This can promote the idea that evidence for God is slowly being eroded by the "pure" truth of science… which is not the case at all.

To help us gain an understanding of the relationship between science and faith, it will be worth having a quick look at history. Apart from anything else, it is a fabulous story!

A whistle-stop tour of the relationship between the biological sciences and faith

The very nature of Christianity has made it particularly receptive to the ideas of science. It provided a nurturing manger within which infant science could mature. It did so because it understood that God was rational and that he had built a rational universe. The very fact that we had physical laws and the mathematical tools that enabled us to study the universe pointed to the reasonableness of this belief. Because God was rational, it was expected that the universe would be understandable. To study his handiwork was to uncover the creativity of God. As such, the act of research could be viewed as an act of worship.

Another reason why Christianity was fruitful to science was its central conviction that God created all things. This meant that none of the things that existed in nature were themselves God. Researchers could therefore investigate, dissect, and codify nature without being impious.

The Italian Dominican friar Thomas Aquinas was an immensely influential philosopher and theologian in the thirteenth century. He was one of the first to articulate the notion of "intelligent design". Aquinas wrote a dissertation in which he gave five proofs of God's existence, known as the "Five Ways". One of these proofs was the complexity of life seen in nature. Aquinas suggested that this complexity indicated that there must have been a designer.

This view held sway for much of history – and still exists today, albeit in a more qualified form.

The fathers of the Reformation in the sixteenth century certainly had a great appreciation of God's handiwork in nature. Martin Luther said, "*All creation is the most beautiful book or Bible; in it God has described and portrayed Himself.*"[3] His counterpart in Switzerland, John Calvin, agreed. He said that nature is "*before our eyes as a most beautiful book in which all created things, whether great or small, are as letters showing the invisible things of God to us*".[4]

Calvin was also helpful in explaining how the creation accounts in the opening chapters of Genesis should be understood. He taught that God has sometimes chosen to accommodate scriptural language so that divine truths can be easily understood by humanity. Calvin therefore agreed with St Augustine that some sections of the Bible are metaphorical.[5] Both Augustine and Calvin were highly critical of those who turned to the Scriptures for answers to cosmological questions that the writers of the Bible never intended to teach. Calvin said, "*He who would learn astronomy and other recondite arts, let him go elsewhere.*"[6]

In the light of this, it is perhaps not surprising that the notion that God could be understood through "two books" – the book of the Bible, and the book of nature – came to be particularly developed in the seventeenth century. Here are some beautiful quotes from that era:

- Francis Bacon (1561–1662), father of scientific reasoning, said that no one "*can search too far, or be too well studied in the book of God's word, or in the book of God's works... but rather, let people endeavour an endless proficience in both*".[7]

- Thomas Browne (1605–82), physician and author, wrote: "*There two books from whence I collect my divinity: besides that written one of God, another of his servant nature... Those that never saw him in the one have discovered him in the other.*"[8]

- The eminent scientist Robert Boyle (1627–91) wrote in a similar way, saying: "*The two great books of nature and scripture have the same author, so the study of the latter does not at all hinder the inquisitive man's delight in the study of the former.*"[9]

This philosophy was shared by Isaac Newton a century later. He was author of the magisterial work *Principia Mathematica,* in which he presented equations that accurately predicted the motions of the planets and the rate at which objects fall to Earth. Newton was motivated to do this research by the thought that it would point people to God. He wrote to his friend, a theologian in Cambridge, saying, "*When I wrote my treatise about our system, I had an eye upon such principles as might work with considering men for the belief of a deity.*"[10]

The argument for the existence of God from the design and complexity of natural things reached its height in the eighteenth century with William Paley. Paley, an English theologian, spoke of the analogy of finding a watch on the ground. Just as no one would seriously consider that the watch had invented itself, no one could reasonably consider that nature, which was infinitely more complex than a watch, could have invented itself. Therefore, nature must have had a designer: God.

Chuck (Charles Darwin)

All this could be believed until the naturalist Charles Darwin (1809–82) popularized a new idea. Darwin travelled the world in a ship called *The Beagle*, collecting and recording information on wildlife and fossils. From what he observed, he concluded that some individuals of a species were able to adapt slightly in a way that made them better able to thrive in a particular environmental niche. Because they were able to thrive, the characteristics that gave them an advantage over other individuals of the same species were passed on to more offspring, causing their numbers to increase. Nature therefore selected the "survival of the fittest". Its continual selection of what worked best ensured that all living species were able to continually adapt and develop so that they became ever more specialized at thriving in a particular ecological environment. This meant that nature did the selection and drove organisms to become more complicated. God was no longer necessary.

Darwin did not grow up with a Christian heritage. He studied theology at Cambridge largely at the insistence of his father after he had failed as a medical student. His father reasoned that if Charles became a Church of England cleric, he would have the time he needed to indulge his naturalist pursuits. Certainly, English clerics were at the forefront of biological research at the time.

Although once kindly disposed to Paley's ideas, Darwin abandoned his nascent Christian faith. He did so for three reasons. The first was his research, which indicated that God did not necessarily intend the existence of specific life forms, as Christianity suggested. The second was the death of his daughter Annie and the suffering he saw in nature. This caused Darwin to struggle with the idea that a loving God existed. (He had a poorly developed theology of suffering.) The third was Darwin's struggle with the idea that God could eternally condemn good people to hell because they weren't Christians.

However, despite walking away from Christianity, Darwin remained a theist. He said, "*I have never been an atheist in the sense of denying the existence of God.*"[11]

Darwin's convictions caused a good deal of consternation in the church, but not universally so. The novelist and cleric Charles Kingsley wrote that he found it "*just as noble a conception of Deity to believe that he created primal forms capable of self-development*".[12] Frederick Temple, the future Archbishop of Canterbury, also preached that "*the finger of God could be seen at work in the laws of nature*", and that there was "*no need to oppose the extension of natural law into new territory*".[13]

Avoiding warfare

If you threaten an ideology or theology that people have used to define their worth, meaning, and identity, you can expect to get your fingers burnt. After all, you are messing with things that are sacred. To suggest that Darwinian thinking fell with barely a ripple on the sensibilities of Western culture, defined in large part by its Christian heritage, would therefore be wrong. Darwin himself was dismayed by the consequences he knew his theory must provoke and this probably caused him some reticence in publishing them. He waited over twenty years after returning to England from his trips abroad before publishing *On the Origin of Species By Means of Natural Selection* in 1859.

Darwin's findings caused a reaction in English society, notwithstanding the prominence of the Church of England with its relatively benevolent and accommodating culture. When that reaction came, it prompted him to reflect wryly, "*Considering how fiercely I have been attacked by the orthodox it seems ludicrous that I once intended to be a clergyman.*"[14] His teaching almost certainly caused him to be denied a knighthood, as some conservative elements in society were affronted by his ideas.[15]

However, it was when Darwin's teachings were used to front atheistic ideology that positions really hardened, triggering an increase in hostilities that is still seen today.

As was mentioned in the last chapter, two people in particular fuelled the idea that there was open warfare between science and Christianity: Andrew White and John Draper. White was the first president of Cornell University, a position he came to at the young age of thirty-three. He refused to impose any religious tests on the students and faculty because he wanted Cornell to be an institution where truth was sought for truth's sake. When pious New Yorkers objected, he hit out at Christianity in a speech given in the great hall of Cooper Union, New York, in 1869. Christianity, he claimed, was inherently antagonistic towards science and had sought to repress science throughout history. Next day, White's speech appeared in the *New York Daily Tribune* under the heading, "The Battle-Fields of Science". White followed this up with a small book entitled *History of the Warfare of Science*. This, in turn, was fleshed out in 1896 with a two-volume work entitled *History of the Warfare of Science with Theology in Christendom*.

The American polymath John Draper echoed White's sentiments in his book *History of the Conflict between Religion and Science* in 1874. Draper's writings were more dogma than reason, but his book was nonetheless a bestseller.

Both White and Draper did much to foster the idea that Christianity is inherently anti-science and that it suppresses truth. Reason and balance became lost amidst the ideological fervour that was generated, and this helped promote the idea that there is an irreconcilable gulf between science and faith.

This is not so.

There are, of course, extremists in both the Christian and scientific world... and it is a fact that any extremism tends to foster an extremist reaction. Sadly, this has happened in the debate about God. Truth, balance, and reason are being torpedoed by the extreme claims of militant atheists on the one hand, and by biblical literalists on the other. So, let's agree to tread between them along the path of truth and reason.

It won't be easy to do so. One of the reasons for this is that many scientists who are experts in their field occasionally allow themselves to be pulled by the gravity field of their own ideology so that they say things that are ideological rather than scientific. So, when the French biologist Jacques Monod says,

> *The ancient covenant is in pieces: man at last knows that he is alone in the unfeeling immensity of the universe, out of which he has emerged only by chance. Neither his destiny nor his duty have been written down...*

he is expressing a personal opinion, not a fact.[16]

The reality is that some of the world's most gifted scientists are saying things that are altogether different from the view expressed by Monod. Francis Collins, who directed the thirteen-year project to map and identify the 25,000 genes of a human being, says, "*I have found there is a wonderful harmony in the complementary truths of science and faith.*"[17]

It is worth noting, in passing, that biologists such as Jacques Monod and Richard Dawkins seem to be particularly attracted to atheism. Perhaps they see the harsh realities of life – the extinctions, predation, and suffering – whereas physicists and mathematicians see more of the beauty and order of the universe.

Tapeworms… and other horrible things

Did God intend every organism, including the tapeworm, to exist? Because if he did, surely this doesn't say much for God's loving and caring nature.

All of us have organisms that we particularly loathe. For David Attenborough, it is the eye worm, loa loa, a parasite that causes blindness and enormous suffering.

Charles Darwin had a particular hatred of the ichneumon wasp. This tiny insect has a needle-like protrusion (called an ovipositor) on the end of its abdomen that it uses to inject eggs into caterpillars. The eggs hatch into maggots that eat their way through the caterpillar, eventually killing it.

These seemingly unpleasant organisms suggest that either God doesn't exist, isn't nice, or has set in place a haphazard universe over which he has no real control.

The idea that God would need to say, "Oops! I didn't really intend the tapeworm to exist, but I guess the giant game of cosmic roulette that I have set up has to allow for it," is not a comforting idea. Nevertheless, it is one that some Christians who are scientists believe.

One of these is John Polkinghorne. He is an Anglican cleric who was once also Professor of Particle Physics at Cambridge University. Polkinghorne says that creation needs to have random acts of chance if it is to develop. In the reproductive cells of animals, for example, mutations can occur quite spontaneously – which may be lethal to them, or alternatively make them better adapted to their environment. He says that God, in his rationality, has created a universe that is able to produce life, but it comes in a package deal that also requires change and risk. We are therefore part of a physical universe

57

that necessarily includes both creativity and danger. God is neither following a rigid blueprint nor abandoning existence to look after itself. The universe, within certain limits, has been encoded by God to make itself and to evolve self-conscious, worshipping beings. Physical evil is the necessary cost of this fruitful complexity.[18]

We shall look more closely at the issue of God and suffering in the next chapter. Two things, however, can be said now.

First, the suggestion that God has set up a giant game of cosmic chance and has no idea what the final outcome will be, is a profoundly unchristian idea (and, to be fair to John Polkinghorne, not one that he supports). Christians understand that God stands outside of time and knows full well what the outcomes of life will be. He fully saw the development of humankind before he began his act of creation. It is therefore logically reasonable to believe that humankind was intended by God even though we know something of the convoluted evolutionary pathway that God has employed to give rise to us.

Secondly, Christians understand that the existence of suffering suggests something is amiss. Suffering is a necessary and temporary condition on the way to the realization of God's wonderful plan. In the meantime, we can know that God shares our pain because of his love, that he has experienced our pain as Jesus, and that he promises to help us in our pain through his empowering Holy Spirit.

If Christianity is right, the really good news is that humanity really was intended to exist. We are not simply the chance winners of an evolutionary game of dice… and that's probably worth a smile.

Intelligent design

If you want to pick a fight with almost anyone, speak about "intelligent design".

The biologist Michael Behe, a biochemist at Lehigh University, Bethlehem, Pennsylvania, is a key proponent of intelligent design. He claims that there are some biological systems, such as the flagellum (a whip-like hair that propels single-celled organisms like bacteria through a liquid medium), which are "irreducibly complex". He points out that the flagellum is made up of forty component parts that form the rotor, stator, U-joint, drive shaft, and propeller of this molecular machine. Behe claims that thirty of these forty components do not exist in any other cellular structures. As all forty pieces are necessary for the flagellum to operate, it is difficult to imagine how the flagellum could have evolved through small modifications that added new parts over time. The component parts would confer no biological advantage until they all existed together and were constructed in a very specific way to form this particular molecular machine. The flagellum is therefore irreducibly complex and shows evidence of intelligent design.

This claim, and others like it, caused a frisson of alarm among humanists and secularists in the Western world. They were terrified that it would lead to schools having to teach children that the Earth was built by God in six days, each twenty-four hours long. The press pounced on it and petitions went flying about, causing people to retreat to their ideological bunkers and poke their tongues out at each other.

The proponents of intelligent design said they were simply putting forward scientific questions, and to stifle such questions would be gagging legitimate enquiry – the very thing that humanists once accused the sixteenth-century Catholic Church of doing.

The humanists pointed out that the motives of those proposing intelligent design would be seen to be more scientifically pure if they were not all solidly in the Christian camp… and so the debate raged on.

It must be said that most biologists and biochemists disagree with Behe and point out that the bacterial flagellum is not irreducibly complex. Nature is filled with examples of precursors to the flagellum that are "missing a part" and yet have a function. For that reason, Behe's argument is not compelling. I have to say, I agree with the majority view. Nature does not show leaps in the organizational structure of living organisms. There are always primitive precursors. Biological development really is a remarkably sequential thing.

It is therefore probably a mistake to look for evidence of God in the intelligent design of organisms. However, it is perfectly valid to see evidence of mind and intention in life generally. As such, scientific atheists need to be careful that they don't point to evolution supposing that, by doing so, they are discrediting the idea of God. While evolution is a very plausible theory that explains the development of biological diversity, it cannot explain why such a mechanism exists, how the universe began, why it is so amazingly ordered… or what life is.

Designed for life

Where does life come from? Where does the life force that is responsible for humour, worship, love, heroism, and creativity originate? What is it? These questions move us well beyond the different evolutionary directions taken by Darwin's finches on the Galapagos Islands. They are "first order" questions.

Some believe that the information responsible for generating life is simply a subset of the laws of physics. It came into being at the very first moment when the universe was born. These laws then dance with chance events, causing life forms to develop… which then continue to evolve in perfectly understandable, scientific ways. They adapt and develop according to the rules of evolution.

Those who believe this do not believe there is any underlying purpose or divine plan.

The trouble with this thinking is that it dodges the question. The all-important issue of what the life force is, in scientific terms, is not answered. Neither does it address the question of how the information codifying the life force is transmitted to an organism. In other words, nothing is put forward scientifically to replace a fairly logical conclusion that there is a mind behind it all: God.

The nervousness of scientists considering the possibility of God is understandable. They don't want to squeeze God into a knowledge gap that perhaps science will later fill. On top of that, the very discipline of science does not allow them to consider non-measurable, non-rational things. They don't have the mandate, methodology, or training to consider issues beyond science. And yet science must inevitably bump up against theology when it considers ultimate causes for the factors that science works with every day. Why is everything so precisely right in the universe to allow life? Why are the workings of the universe so transparent to us? What is life… and where does it come from? In other words, it is a perfectly rational thing to ask why the universe appears shot through with signs of mind.

The problem is, having postulated the possibility of God for rational reasons, there is no scientific way of testing it. Scientists therefore come up against a boundary. The fact that most of them then back away from that boundary to address propositions that they can test and examine with experiments, does not disprove God. It is simply that scientists don't have the tools or language to explore the possibility of God.

Reason suggests it is perfectly rational to believe there may be a mind behind the life force seen in nature. For those atheists who are scientists and who want to define their identity in purely rationalist terms, this is deeply disturbing. They want rationalism to provide all the answers. As such, they tend to shrug and claim that, given enough time, there will be a way of explaining everything rationally.

They are drawing a lot of money on a fairly blank cheque.

Some scientists believe there is evidence that life is written into the laws of physics. The American chemist Sidney Fox has claimed that the laws responsible for the formation of peptide bonds in the production of proteins will automatically cause life to develop in the same way that water inevitably forms ice crystals when the temperature drops.[19] Fox believes that life spontaneously generates under the right physical conditions – when inorganic molecules form amino acids that join together to form amino acid polymers (which he calls "proteinoides").[20]

This is not convincing. Life is not just a mechanical thing; it also has a great deal to do with information. There is no evidence to suggest that amino acids contain the information necessary to confer life. Complexifying amino acids into proteinoides is simply chemistry; it doesn't explain life any more than sticking pages into a book explains reading.

If life were an unremarkable product of chemistry, we would reasonably expect life to pop up everywhere in the universe where there was a life-friendly environment. The Belgian biochemist

Christian De Duve is one who believes there must be many celestial bodies in our universe with a similar history to Earth and therefore a great number of opportunities for life to exist. Accordingly, he doesn't believe that life on Earth is particularly special or unlikely.[21]

The rather obvious caution regarding De Duve's thinking is that life has not been found anywhere else in the universe… and may never be found.

His thinking does mean, however, that there is quite a lot at stake, both theologically and scientifically, over whether or not life exists elsewhere in the universe.

Life on other planets

The American Congress doesn't believe there is extraterrestrial intelligence in the universe – certainly not in any form that is worth looking for. It quashed NASA's SETI (Search for Extraterrestrial Intelligence) programme in 1993. NASA is now focusing on SETL (the Search for Extraterrestrial Life).

Scientists are searching our galaxy for habitable zones that exist around a star where planets or moons have an atmosphere capable of supporting liquid water on their surface. They are looking for zones which are "just right" for planets within them to support life. These areas have come to be known colloquially as "Goldilocks zones".

Numerous planets in such zones have now been discovered. Most are bigger than Earth, simply because the bigger planets are easier to detect. On 4 November 2013, astronomers reported that data from the Kepler space mission suggests there could be as many as 40 billion Earth-sized planets orbiting in the habitable zones of stars (both red dwarf stars and normal stars).

That's a lot.

But we still haven't found extraterrestrial life. That doesn't mean it's not there; it's simply a reflection of how hard it is to discover when the distances involved are so huge and the number of solar systems is so large. Interestingly enough, the search parameters for life have recently been expanded because evidence of substantial amounts of water has been found outside the Goldilocks zones on planets and moons sustained by radioactive decay and other forms of energy.

Discoveries such as these prompt us to consider what the significance would be of finding life on other planets.

The answer is not at all clear. If life were only found on planet Earth, it would cause us to wonder why Earth should be so special. It would certainly prompt us to consider the possibility that a divine mind intended us to exist.

If, on the other hand, life is found to be abundant in the universe, this might suggest that De Duve is right and life is not special or purposed. It is simply the inevitable product of chemical reactions that occur widely throughout the universe.

Alternatively, it might suggest that life was intended by God and that he designed the universe to allow it to occur everywhere. If this were so, and sentient life were discovered on other planets, this could be problematic for Christians because it would challenge their understanding of the unique status of humankind.

Be that as it may, no life has yet been found beyond planet Earth. Therefore, to build an atheistic philosophy that depends on life being "unspecial" and common in the universe would be premature and quite possibly wrong.

Judging by the way things appear now, the shadow of God can be seen both in nature and in the miracle of life.

The cleverness of death

We have spoken about the extraordinary and unlikely phenomenon of life – something that justifiably requires an explanation. However, it is worth pointing out that death is also something to wonder at. Its existence is very clever and the fact that it does exist should not be taken for granted.

For nature to exist as it does, there must be a mechanism that allows life and a mechanism that allows death. Both have to exist to allow the evolutionary process to work. All living organisms need to have built-in obsolescence. Older generations need to offer their genetic characteristics for selection by a local environment to see which characteristics result in more successful offspring. After they have done this, they need to oblige the system by getting out of the way; that is, by dying.

Death is therefore a very essential and rather clever idea. For life to exist, living things need to be engineered in such a way that they have to die.

Circling herring gulls and fishy things

We have been speaking a lot about evolution. Some people in the Christian church have suggested that, while they accept that an organism can change in order to adapt to different environments, they struggle to believe organisms can actually evolve into new species.

The short answer to this is that they can. First, though, it might be helpful to remind ourselves what the process of evolution is. Evolution is a process of genetic change in an organism that helps it to thrive in its particular ecological niche so that it produces more offspring. Generation by generation, changes can occur that make a species more or less likely to succeed. Nature selects those changes that make an organism more fit to survive. As a general rule, taxonomists (scientists who name and categorize living organisms) declare that an organism has evolved into a new species when it has changed so much that it can no longer mate with its original parent species.

Numerous accounts of speciation (the development of new species) exist. Here's one about herring gulls.

Seven discrete populations of *Larus spp.* (the genus of the herring gull and black-backed gull) are found around the edge of the Arctic. Populations of *Larus* changed over the years as they migrated around the edge of the Arctic until the resultant species had changed so much that its adults could no longer mate with the original parent species.

This is just one of a number of examples which indicate that evolution is both observable and measurable.

Evolution is a very powerful mechanism that allows for the diversification and development of life. There are some amazing examples of this. A favourite for the American biologist Stephen Gould is a freshwater mussel called *Lampsilis*. This mussel lies partly buried in the bottom of lakes and has a structure on its protruding end that looks exactly like a little fish. It has side flaps, a tail, a streamlined body, and an eyespot. The flaps even undulate in a swimming motion. When a real fish comes to investigate it, the mussel discharges its larvae, some of which find their way onto the fish's gills where they continue to develop inside cysts. When the larvae mature, the cysts rupture, releasing the *Lampsilis* to the lake floor where they complete their adult life.[22]

It is extraordinary to consider that evolution should be responsible for such an exquisite mechanism.

Doing justice to the facts

If science claims to have the sole prerogative on knowledge, it will preserve its empirical chastity but risk trapping itself in an empiricist prison of its own making. This is quite okay if scientists are content to restrict their comments to science, but when atheistic scientists claim a scientific mandate for scorning the idea of God, then they are asking things of science that it simply can't deliver. There are huge restraints on what scientists can validly say about God from a scientific perspective. God, almost by definition, has to be beyond the ability of scientists to investigate, quantify, and codify. This doesn't mean that God doesn't exist; it simply means that scientists don't have the language to make a judgment about God other than to suspect his existence on the basis of what they observe.

The genius of God, it seems, is that he chooses to be known as much by a child wondering at the night sky as by a scientist mapping the human genome.

Without God, things become logically difficult. Atheists have to look at a world riddled with order and codes and say that it all comes from nothing as a result of mechanisms that are not known. All the atheist can do is reach for the "infinite" escape clause and say that life has arisen because there are an infinite number of universes that exist, and therefore it is not surprising that at least one of them has stumbled on the ability to synthesize life. Chance alone has resulted in a species that is able to value love, justice, altruism, self-sacrifice, music, humour, and art.

This is not a satisfactory argument. Chance may determine where a particular football player stands on a playing field at any one time, but it doesn't explain why the football team is on the playing field.

It is difficult to avoid the suspicion that such atheistic thinking has arisen from ideological preconceptions rather than from facts. Atheism is a conviction that atheists bring *to* science; it is not one that they get *from* science.

Christians, on the other hand, look at the marvels of life and say that what they see is consistent with the idea of God. What they observe convinces them that belief in God is reasonable.

Dispensing with creation like a badly made pot

I have been making the case that there is evidence of God in nature. Life, in all its hues, is an extraordinary and highly unlikely thing. While its form can be explained scientifically, its existence cannot.

So, what is it that Christians believe about life, nature, and the universe? What are God's intentions for it?

Christianity teaches that God will eventually bring this imperfect universe to an end so that he can renew it, combine it with a new heaven, and inaugurate the kingdom of God – the final realization of his purposes.

If this is so, a question that might reasonably be asked is: If God's creation is so special, why does Christianity teach that God will remake it as a potter might remake a flawed shape on his wheel? Should we expect to see God's handiwork in nature if it is so flawed? Should we really consider nature to be special?

Yes, we should.

Christians are supposed to care for the environment and for the creation around them for two very good reasons. The first is that God made it, values it, and instructs us to care for it. The second is that God will pattern his future kingdom on aspects of our present existence. As such, it makes no sense to desecrate that pattern. Yes, everything will change with the inauguration of God's new kingdom, but this doesn't mean that the coming kingdom has no continuity with our present creation. The Bible speaks of creation waiting to be redeemed... and of us being transformed (Romans 8:20–23; 1 Corinthians 15:51). The one verse that does suggest complete annihilation of the Earth is 2 Peter 3:10. Properly understood though, this verse speaks of the destruction of the Earth in terms of the judgment of sin. It goes on to say that all will be "laid bare"; in other words, uncovered and put on show to display what it really is.

We get a clue about the continuing yet transformed nature of God's coming kingdom in the nature of Jesus' resurrected body. The first thing to note is that he was no vapid ghost. The resurrected Jesus was real and could be touched. He was, however, different in that he wasn't always recognized by his disciples and he wasn't restricted by some of our physical laws. He could, for example, enter a room with locked doors (John 20:19).

The Apostle Paul describes the difference between our current earthly body and our future spiritual body by saying that our earthly body is like a seed, pregnant with the possibilities of God – which only realizes its full potential when it is transformed into its intended goal and becomes a magnificent, mature plant (1 Corinthians 15:42–44).

The significance of this is that we should not scorn this present creation. It has continuity with the kingdom to come. That kingdom will be the full realization of God's intentions for all that he has made. It is little wonder, then, that the Apostle Paul speaks in Romans 8:22–23 of all creation longing to be renewed.

These motives are enough for me to care for the environment. I respect God's creation because God made it and told us to take care of it.

And because God made it, I am not surprised to see evidence of his handiwork in it.

The need for both science and theology

Both science and theology are necessary. Theology asks if there is more to be understood about science's laws of nature than the simple fact that they exist. It goes beyond the realm of empirical fact to address questions such as why things are as they are.

Because science and theology are different ways of knowing truth, they have the ability to inform and constrain each other so that each becomes the other's moderator and mentor. Without science, theology can become polluted with illogical dogma. Without theology, science will struggle to make sense of existence and people's experience of the spiritual. Fraser Watts, Professor of Science and Theology at Cambridge, says:

> *Science and religion cannot be confined to their separate compartments and ignore each other. They are each concerned with truth and there cannot be multiple truths which are completely unconnected with each other.*[23]

It is therefore important to allow both disciplines. If science allows theology, it might surprise itself by discovering the "why" behind the "what". Some scientific disciplines, such as cosmology, are already pushing up against metaphysical questions. The astronomer and physicist Robert Jastrow makes this point when he says:

> *At this moment, it seems as though science will never be able to raise the curtain on the mystery of creation. For the scientist who has lived by his faith in the power of reason, the story ends like a bad dream. He has scaled the mountains of ignorance; he is about to conquer the highest peak; as he pulls himself over the final rock, he is greeted by a band of theologians who have been sitting there for centuries.*[24]

Made in the image of God

God says in Genesis 1:26, "*Let us make mankind in our image, in our likeness.*" What does this mean?

I suggest that it means the following:

- The big-heartedness of God lives in us.
- The passion for good to win lives in us.
- The creativity of God lives in us.
- The desire for significance lives in us.
- The ache for the love of God lives in us.
- The hunger for the eternity of God lives in us.

It also explains why:

- death is obscene to us;
- lack of meaning is obscene to us;
- lack of relationships is obscene to us;
- lack of a purpose is obscene to us;
- lack of being able to give and receive love is obscene to us.

All this makes sense if we are made in God's image as spiritual beings.

Christians believe that we are the result of a deliberate act of self-expression on the part of God. We are made in his image. This is profound. No other religion in the history of the world has made this claim.

Being made in the image of God means we have the ability to make spiritual, intellectual, and moral judgments in a way that no other created animal can – even those to which we are closely related biologically. Dr Ian Tattersall, in his book, *Becoming*

Human, says that humanity represents a totally unprecedented entity on Earth.[25]

Being made in the image of God also means we are sacred. We are therefore not free to abuse, kill, exploit, or hate each other. If we are unsure how to behave or how we should express ourselves as those who bear God's image, we have a fabulous role model in Jesus.

The clues God has left us in nature concerning his existence indicate that he wants us to find him. He wants to be found, but he leaves room for our cooperation. He wants to be known, but he leaves room for faith. He wants to be obvious, but not so obvious as to compel faith. Rather, he invites faith.

God has done everything in his power to suggest his existence without compelling us to believe in him. He has created a universe so finely tuned that it not only allows life; it allows life that is self-conscious, that laughs, that composes symphonies, that paints like Monet and Renoir, that writes like Shakespeare, that feels compassion like Mother Teresa, and that is heroic like Jesus. The miracle is not just that we exist, but it's the manner in which we exist.

God wants to be found in nature. The Bible says, *"The heavens declare the glory of God; the skies proclaim the work of his hands"* (Psalm 19:1). It also says, *"God's invisible qualities – his eternal power and divine nature – have been clearly seen, being understood from what has been made"* (Romans 1:20).

Clearly, God expects something of his identity to be known from what exists in nature, even if the natural world has been corrupted by sin and suffering.

Why has God left clues about himself in nature?

Because he wants to be found.

3

THE EVIDENCE OF GOD IN SUFFERING

This chapter is very different from the first two in that we will be looking at theology; specifically, the Christian understanding of suffering.

Suffering is a big deal. It has huge implications for what people believe about God. I once conducted a survey among 311 tertiary-trained people and discovered that 41 per cent of them believed that the incidence of suffering in the world suggests no loving God is in control.[1]

The trouble is, atheism does not provide a convincing alternative. When considering the extraordinary features of the cosmos and nature, the atheist has to believe that existence, order, and sentient life have no significance. They are meaningless.

Another unavoidable belief that atheists must hold is that there is no ultimate justice. This, of course, doesn't prove that atheism is wrong; it is simply a logical consequence of its philosophy. The scary thing about this, as history attests, is that such a position cannot help but have implications for the moral behaviour of society. (This will be explored later in Chapter 5.)

Evangelastics

Atheists scorn the idea of the miraculous – particularly when it comes to claims of divine healing. Some of this is deserved. Christianity has not been helped by exaggerated claims of some falsely spiritual people. So, as an aside, can I gently ask these people to be careful with God's reputation? God does not require "evangelastics" (a stretching of the truth for the sake of evangelism) from anyone. He is a God of integrity and truth.

Placing limits on God

In the previous chapter, I alluded to the danger of scientists locking themselves into an empiricist prison in which their view of truth is limited. (An empiricist is a person who will not believe anything to be true unless it has been shown to be so experimentally.) One symptom of this limited vision is seen when an empiricist grudgingly allows for the possibility that God is responsible for the universe… but then insists that God abandon his creation and leave the rest to chance.

This displays a curious and inconsistent logic. It allows God to create, but doesn't allow him to stand outside of time and know full well what sentient life will occur. Those who believe this have a very inadequate view of God. They want to saddle him with human limitations such as not being able to know the future.

The fact is that if God exists, a great deal more is possible. However, this doesn't mean that everything is possible. God, after all, is rational and has chosen to work through our history. As such, only those actions ascribed to God that have historical and logical credibility are valid. We are not free to believe that God has made tiny planets in the shape of teapots to circle the Sun.

If God exists and has come to us as Jesus Christ, then it is logically possible for the events recorded in the Gospels to have happened. Indeed, it makes them very likely. So, while God chooses never to be so obvious as to compel faith – and while God normally chooses to work through the laws of nature that he has put in place – he is under no obligation to adhere to the empiricist's dictum: "Nothing supernatural here, please."

74

When this is understood, it becomes possible to allow God to let you see further than the prison walls of empiricism. It becomes possible to see the resurrection of Jesus from the dead as something necessary and logical. Nothing else was going to show us that death doesn't have the last word. Nothing else was going to cause us to believe that resurrection life is possible. It was God's peerless "show and tell". Nothing else was going to cause us to take seriously God's plan to end this imperfect world and inaugurate his eternal kingdom.

All this has huge relevance for our ability to see evidence of God's existence, reason, and character in the Bible's teaching on the hardest subject that exists in the world: suffering.

Looking for clues

If God exists, it will be almost impossible to believe that he has not left clues about himself and his purpose in this key area. Just as importantly, if it can be shown that the Bible's teaching on suffering is unusable, simplistic, inadequate, or untrue, we can dismiss the idea of God. However, if biblical teaching on suffering gives the fullest and most satisfying answers possible, the signs are good that God exists.

Nothing sorts out the validity of philosophies and religions like the issue of suffering.

The Hindu Vedas teach that suffering is an illusion. We must faithfully live out our status in life and earn the right to a better life at our next reincarnation.

Buddhists say that suffering comes as a result of desire. We must therefore kill off all desire and work towards escaping this world so that we become subsumed into nothingness.

Many other religions say that bad things happen to people because they are bad. Humanists say there is no reason, no meaning, no God, and no hope. Therefore, just get on and live life as pragmatically as possible.

I have to confess that on the basis of what I observe in life, I don't find these philosophies persuasive or helpful. They call to mind a story:

> *There was once a young man who fell into a pit with walls so steep that he couldn't get out. Leaders of several of the world's religions came to the edge of the pit and said that if the man had behaved better and been wiser, he wouldn't have fallen into the pit. After they left, a New Age devotee came and said to the man that if he closed his eyes and practised transcendental meditation, he could pretend the pit wasn't there. The next person who came to the edge of the pit was a postmodernist. He called down to the imprisoned man and told him that he had a valid lifestyle and had obviously been liberated from the shackles of conventionalism by being in the pit. Meanwhile, the man remained trapped in the pit.*

The question is: Can Christianity fare any better? Can we see evidence of God in his teaching on suffering? Does Christianity make sense of what we see in life and address adequately the full complexities of this difficult subject?

In exploring whether we can see evidence of God in suffering, I don't just want to explore the claim that Christianity makes suffering people happy. Plenty of deluded people are happy. Neither am I content to prove that if anyone can attribute meaning to suffering, this will take its power away.

Viktor Frankl, a psychiatrist who survived the Holocaust,

says that if you manage to find meaning in your suffering, you will be able to bear it bravely and honourably. Finding meaning in suffering takes its tyrannical power away so that its strident demands for you to be miserable and self-obsessed are broken.[2]

While this makes good psychological sense, I want to go beyond helping you to adjust your thinking so that you can feel happier. I want to ask two questions that are infinitely more significant: What is *true* about suffering? And can anything about God be learned through suffering?

The motorbike shop

Many years ago, when I was a minister in a country town, I rode a motorbike. I used to hang out with a bunch of local bike riders behind the motorbike shop for "happy hour" on Friday evenings. On one such occasion, I had ridden in from out of town and was wearing my bike jacket. The relevance of this was that I wasn't looking much like a church minister.

A man I'd not met before was part of the group at the workshop and it was obvious that he was angry. He was effing and blinding to anyone who would listen. The rest of the guys let him go on like this until one of them told him I was a church minister. It took a while for him to believe it. When he did, he said, "I don't believe in God. I used to, but then I went to Vietnam and got badly wounded. God didn't look after me at all."

I had every sympathy with the bloke and said, "I don't blame you. I wouldn't believe in that god either."

He was rather puzzled and thought I probably should, given that I was a church minister.

"No," I said. "You believed in a god who was a good luck charm. So when your good luck charm didn't work, you threw it away. Very sensible."

He looked bewildered, so I went on.

"But if you are interested in meeting the one true God – the God who loves you, who died for you, and who said he would never leave you, even in the bad times… if you are interested in the God who said that Christians are not immune to suffering, but would be persecuted like he was… if you are interested in the God who calls us to be faithful and to work with him on a project to defeat sin and suffering… then, yes," I said, "I'd be happy to talk with you about that God – the God who actually exists."

I know a lot of people who scorn Christianity because of some tragedy in their family. They were looking for a "sugar daddy" god. But God is not that. He never has been. Even a cursory look at the lives of holy men and women in the Bible makes this clear. Horrendous things happened to them. God did not spare them from suffering. He did, however, lift them above the suffering so that it did not have the final authority in their life.

Avoidable suffering

From time to time, I conduct funerals. On such occasions, I'm often asked, "Why did this have to happen to our loved one? He/She was such a good person." The implication, of course, is that God is unfair because bad things should only happen to bad people.

This idea has existed through much of history and still exists today. It was, in fact, so popular in Jesus' time that he needed to address it.

The real difficulty with this understanding is that it is not entirely wrong. We are all guilty of sin, and we all continue to fall short of God's standards of holiness in some way. We all make poor choices occasionally, and these choices have consequences for our lives. The Old Testament book of Proverbs tells us how life works best most of the time. It says that ungodly, unwise behaviour generally results in suffering. Accordingly, it invites us to avoid needless suffering caused by:

- mere talk and no action (Proverbs 14:23; 28:19);
- pride (Proverbs 13:10);
- choosing not to be guided by wisdom (Proverbs 4:6; 22:3; 27:12);
- hate (Proverbs 10:12);
- sexual immorality (Proverbs 6:28–29);
- laziness (Proverbs 6:6–11);
- lack of generosity (Proverbs 21:13; 28:27);
- developing a hot temper (Proverbs 22:24–25);
- being greedy (Proverbs 23:4–5; 25:16);
- drunkenness (Proverbs 23:20–21, 29–32);
- being a busybody (Proverbs 26:17);
- concealing sin (Proverbs 28:13);
- failing to discipline your child (Proverbs 29:17).

Christianity acknowledges the obvious truth that some suffering is caused by our own unwise choices. However, while this is true, it in no way explains all suffering.

Do bad things only happen to bad people?

The belief that all suffering is caused by the victim living a bad life is a cruel and unjust one. Jesus crashes against this simplistic thinking in his teaching, recorded in Luke 13:1–5. Some people (who were probably aware of Jesus' Galilean accent) had told Jesus of a time when Pontius Pilate killed some Galileans in the temple court. Perhaps those telling Jesus this were trying to warn him to be careful. Alternatively, they might have been implying that since Galileans were notorious for causing political trouble, it served them right. (Galilee was well north of the political and religious centre, Jerusalem, and Galileans often resented its control.)

Jesus reminded those with whom he was speaking of the eighteen people who died when a tower fell on them. As this occurred near the pool of Siloam in their own sacred city of Jerusalem, the victims could in no way be considered northern troublemakers. So, how did Jesus make sense of this needless death, a tragic accident which had nothing to do with people's poor choices?

Jesus made it plain that those who suffered and died were not necessarily more evil than others. He taught that their suffering was one of the sad consequences of the rejection of God by *all* people, and of the world's choice to go down a path that God never intended. As such, suffering points to the need for all of us to turn to God and seek his forgiveness.

This teaching makes sense. It in no way supports the silly idea that only evil people suffer. Jesus' teaching points to the reality that life is inherently "spoiled". He highlights the responsibility we all have to cooperate with God so that things can be restored.

The universe is a good thing spoiled

At the start of the Bible, we read the story of Adam and Eve and how their disobedience resulted in the land being cursed (Genesis 3:17–19). This is not just a fanciful story. It established a principle that played out repeatedly in the history of Israel: rebellion against God results in good land becoming wasteland (Psalm 107:33–34; Jeremiah 9:12–13; Hosea 4:1–3). In a very real sense, it can be said that sin defiled the land and brought suffering (Isaiah 24:4–6; Jeremiah 2:7).

I say this to underline the fact that some suffering can be avoided by living as God intends. The Apostle Peter certainly knew this. He taught that no Christian should ever suffer as a result of folly or a lack of integrity (1 Peter 4:15).

What does this mean?

It means that the only suffering Christians can escape is that which can be avoided by good and wise behaviour.

Some suffering, however, is not avoidable. Earthquakes and tsunamis have made this very clear.

Christians are not immune to suffering caused by the accidents and incidents of life. If they were, people would become Christians just to stop bad things happening to them. This would mean that Christianity wouldn't be the free choice that God wants it to be. Christians have to be subject to the same rhythms and vagaries of life as non-Christians (Matthew 5:45). Certainly, Jesus did not mince his words about the realities of hardship in this life. He said, "*In this world you will have trouble*" (John 16:33), so don't expect that you won't.

This does not mean, however, that we are forced to lie helplessly in the jaws of suffering, overwhelmed by evil while we wait for "pie in the sky when we die". Christians are ambassadors for God's kingdom. We are a people commissioned by God to prefigure the kingdom of God by displaying the love and truth of God. Christians are those who are being transformed by God's Spirit so that they have the compassion to address evil and suffering wherever they see it.

But we should never expect this to be easy. Christians live in an alien environment in which they will not only experience the inherent dangers of life, but also persecution (John 15:20;

1 Thessalonians 3:2–4). All Christians are called to carry the light of God's truth and grace in a world that prefers darkness (Matthew 5:15). Life for Christians, more than anyone else, is neither fair nor easy. Jesus pointed out that if he was persecuted, his followers have no right to expect anything different (John 15:20).

This sobering reminder prevents Christians from spiralling off into a poorly founded "success theology" where they believe that because they are Christians, they will be immune to grief, hardship, and suffering.

It's worth pausing here to ask the question: How is God shaping up? Does his teaching (as recorded in the Bible) stack up against your experience of suffering? Does it have the ring of truth? I hope you are finding that it does. However, there are a lot more questions still to answer, so let's continue.

Honouring God in suffering

As I ponder the extraordinary aversion to suffering of today's Western church, with its misguided sense that it has some sort of divine right to a pain-free, blessed life, I can't help but contrast it with the teaching of Scripture and the attitude of the early church.

Jesus says consistently in Scripture that those who lose their life for his sake will find it (Matthew 10:38–39; 16:24–25; Luke 9:24). This understanding led the early church to believe that it was a privilege to suffer for Christ. If you are in any doubt about this, read what Ignatius of Antioch wrote while on his way to martyrdom in Rome (early in the second century).

The early Christians understood that suffering brought about by the mere fact they were disciples of Christ meant that they were sharing in the sufferings of Christ (Colossians 1:24). They considered this to be a privilege... and something that would be rewarded in God's kingdom (Matthew 5:11–12; James 1:2–4).

Certainly, God is honoured when we are faithful in the midst of our suffering. This was the case with Job in the Old Testament. Job remained faithful despite the worst that evil could throw at him. His faithfulness in the face of suffering showed the spiritual realms of evil that God had given him the strength to stand strong and be victorious.[3]

The sort of faith that allows us to trust God in times of suffering is the greatest compliment anyone can give to God. Job had this faith – faith that enabled him to say, "*Though he slay me, yet will I hope in him*" (Job 13:15).

Now that's a faith that God can throw in Satan's face!

The question I want to ask is this: Why was it that people in the Bible could cheerfully embrace martyrdom, while the Western church today expects God to bless it in every way?

Let's join the early church at Bible school and discover some of the secrets they knew.

What does the Bible teach?

Essentially, the Bible teaches us that suffering comes from two sources. First, it is a temporary expression of a broken universe that is being driven by laws that have been corrupted by sin. Nature, as well as humankind, is waiting to be made new (Romans 8:18–22). The corruption of the laws of nature explains natural evil such as tsunamis and diseases.

Secondly, the Bible teaches that suffering is a consequence of people's choice to embrace evil. Their freedom to do so explains why moral evil exists.

So, what are we to make of the fact that these sources of suffering exist? Where is God in it all?

The early Christians understood that even in the midst of suffering, God was not absent. He knew the number of hairs on their head (Matthew 10:30) and every detail of their circumstances. He cared about those who suffered, and promised to be with them. He was able to identify fully with them because he himself had suffered as Jesus. This meant that while they knew they might not be saved from hardships, they would never have to face their trials alone. Jesus would never forsake them and, if invited, would walk with them through life, lending them his strength (Matthew 28:18–20; Hebrews 13:5).

It's worth remembering that God has chosen never to allow his authority to be entirely absent from any situation of suffering. Even in the vilest cases of suffering caused by evil, the voice of God, however small, can be heard giving the strength to endure, the ability to tell others about Jesus, and the courage to bring reform. This is what Christians can throw in the face of evil.

Not only will God never let his voice be entirely absent in any scenario of suffering, he sometimes (note: *sometimes*) chooses to turn the suffering into something that can be used for his purposes. God once allowed a man to be sick so that Jesus could do a work of healing that would glorify God's name (John 9:1–3). On another occasion, Paul's imprisonment in Rome resulted in his military jailers learning about Jesus (Philippians 1:12–13).

The one thing the early church particularly understood was that this life is not all there is. Their hope was in the future kingdom of God. As such, this was the kingdom in which they invested (Matthew 6:19–21).

The Bible teaches that God is honoured when people stay faithful to him in the midst of their suffering (Job 1:8–12; 2:3–6; Ephesians 3:10). Such faithfulness bears witness to all those who are watching that God can be honoured by Christians despite the worst that Satan throws at them. Showing that you trust God despite your suffering is the greatest compliment anyone can give to God (Job 13:15). As we read before, the early disciples understood that suffering for God was a privilege (Acts 5:41; Philippians 1:29; 3:10; 1 Peter 4:12–13). It allowed them to suffer with Jesus, and so share with him in his epic plan to rescue humanity back to himself.

I can't help but notice that, while the Western church has tried to advance the gospel using the tool of commercial success, the New Testament church advanced the gospel through suffering (Colossians 1:24). The early Christians understood that being "in Christ" meant sharing in his death, in his Spirit, in his holiness, in his resurrection, and, for a short time, in his suffering. The Apostle Paul couldn't imagine that anyone could have the Spirit of Christ in them without being prepared to share in Christ's sufferings (Romans 8:16–17).

While this is so, it is important to remember that the early Christians were not spiritual masochists. Neither did they consider themselves to be helpless in the face of suffering. They attacked suffering and injustice with the love and power of God whenever they could, for this was exactly what Jesus did. He saw suffering as a form of evil, something to be overcome. Jesus sought to liberate people from all that oppressed them (Luke 4:16–21). He healed those who were sick (Matthew 8:16) and commanded his disciples to do the same using the authority of his name (Matthew 10:1).

Christians, therefore, are called to combat suffering wherever they see it.

Can suffering be explained as something that allows a "greater good"?

If you said to a woman who'd had her children murdered in a Nazi concentration camp that it happened because God was pursuing a greater good, you would justifiably earn her anger and scorn.

A lot more needs to be said.

Let's proceed carefully and acknowledge that *some* suffering is necessary for us to live life well. If we felt no pain, our bodies wouldn't be able to tell us when they were damaged. We need pain to prompt us to move when we are too close to a fire. But even so, this argument is not sufficient to explain the hideous pain that goes well beyond biological necessity.

The Bible teaches that pain is not only necessary for biological reasons, it also helps us mature in character and faith so that we are able to cope with the rigours of life. James writes in the Bible, saying:

> *Consider it pure joy, my brothers and sisters, whenever*
> *you face trials of many kinds, because you know that*
> *the testing of your faith produces perseverance. Let*
> *perseverance finish its work so that you may be mature*
> *and complete, not lacking anything.*
>
> (James 1:2–4)

The Apostle Paul understood this. He taught that he and his colleagues had endured great suffering in order to learn not to rely on themselves but on God (2 Corinthians 1:8–9). Still later, he went on to explain why God had not healed him of a condition that vexed him greatly. It was to prevent him from becoming too conceited as a result of the special insight and revelation that God had given him (2 Corinthians 12:7–10).

Paul does assure us, however, that suffering need not have the last word (Romans 5:3–4). He promises that if we persevere, we will grow a godly character. When we notice our character changing, we can be encouraged and see it as evidence that God's

Holy Spirit is at work within us. This, in turn, gives us hope that God is getting us ready for his kingdom.

So there it is: Suffering can result in perseverance, which can result in character, which can result in hope.

But while there are some positive sides to pain, this does not explain all pain. It does not justify torture chambers, the deaths of millions of people in plagues, or the genocide perpetrated by evil regimes. These cannot be adequately explained by saying that God has allowed it to facilitate a greater good.

So, let's dig deeper.

Is there anything to be discovered by exploring the relationship between theology's understanding of suffering and science's understanding of suffering?

How does the Christian understanding of suffering dance with science?

I am sometimes saddened by the uneven alliance that occurs between science and theology at many science/faith conferences. Too often, theology struggles to contribute much to the debate at all. Delegates seem to be content to argue the case that faith is scientifically credible – and leave it at that.

However, when it comes to suffering, this won't do. If the only voice heard in discussions about suffering is that of science, then the only conclusion to be reached is that this universe of pain was the best God could do if he wanted to build a self-sustaining universe able to produce sentient life.

More needs to be said.

Is a suffering universe the best God could do?

Arthur Peacocke, Ian Barbour, and John Polkinghorne are three theologians with a distinguished scientific background. They each speak of the need for the universe to be able to generate authentic novelty in order to allow its fruitfulness to be explored. Peacocke stresses the essential role of chance in the development of the universe's potentialities. He points out that God creates through the interaction of physical laws and chance. God does not direct events by occasionally poking his fingers into gaps in the process.[4] God is present within the epic of evolution, but chooses to work within normal laws of nature. However, the cost of evolutionary complexity is pain and suffering, for an evolutionary world must involve both predation and death. It is a cost that God is prepared to sanction in order for him to have a fruitful universe.[5]

Ian Barbour has largely adopted the philosophy of process theology. Accordingly, he thinks slightly differently. He suggests that the universe is incomplete and is still coming into being.[6] God is not responsible for suffering because he is committed to working with us in a consensual, communal relationship. This means that he will seek to persuade, rather than coerce, existence along certain pathways. When the world fails to go down these pathways, God shares in the resultant suffering with us. Barbour goes on to say that the emergence of higher levels of consciousness will inevitably result in a greater capacity for suffering. However, this is not a bad thing, as suffering contributes to moral growth (Romans 5:3).[7] Courage would be impossible without danger and temptation... and the opportunity to choose good would be meaningless without the opportunity to choose evil.

John Polkinghorne seeks to steer between the idea that God has love without power (he is an impotent spectator) and the contrasting idea that God has power without love (he is a cosmic tyrant). He suggests that God interacts with creation, but chooses not to overrule its divinely granted freedom to be itself. Created order is a package deal that includes creativity, change, and risk. For example, mutations can occur spontaneously in the reproductive cells of animals which may either be lethal to them or cause them to be better adapted to their environment. The same biochemical processes that enable cells to mutate, making evolution possible, are those that enable cells to become cancerous and generate tumours. You cannot have one without the other. We are part of a physical universe with all its inherent creativity and danger. God is neither following a rigid blueprint nor abandoning existence to look after itself. Rather, he has encoded the universe to develop itself and evolve self-conscious, worshipping beings. Physical suffering and evolutionary blind alleys are the necessary cost of this fruitful complexity.[8]

Francis Collins, who led the international team that decoded the human genome, agrees. He says:

> *The consequences of the evolutionary process are, admittedly, at times, things which cause suffering for individuals even today. A child with cancer may well be seen as one of those side effects of the fact that DNA copying is not perfect. It's important that DNA copying not be perfect or evolution wouldn't be possible.*

He goes on to say with masterful understatement, *"but if it results in a cancer arising in a child, isn't that a terrible price to pay? These are difficult questions to be sure."*[9]

Something of the inadequacy of explaining suffering from a purely scientific perspective is acknowledged by Denis Alexander, former Director of the Faraday Institute for Science and Religion at St Edmund's College, Cambridge. *"These are not the kind of reflections that are likely to be of much help to someone actually passing through a period of suffering,"* he writes. But then he adds optimistically, *"... although they might be."* He sees enough merit in the suffering-is-the-inevitable-consequence-of-God-making-a-self-evolving-universe hypothesis to suggest that it may give some comfort in times of suffering.[10]

I have to be honest and say that in all my years of ministry, I have yet to find anyone who has derived any comfort from this philosophy. I am left with the feeling that it is not enough. While it takes cognizance of the scientific evidence, it offers little from a theological position.

Can anything more helpful be said?

God isn't to blame; he doesn't know the future

In recent decades, a new proposal for understanding the nature of God has been advanced. It is variously known as the "open view of God", "free will theism", or "open theism". Open theism (popularized by theologians such as Clark Pinnock, John Sanders, and Greg Boyd) proposes that God has chosen to limit his power so that he is able to engage in a reciprocal way with people on a day-to-day level.[11] Our poor choices, and God's limited power, have resulted in the suffering we experience.

Open theism says that God has not locked everything into place by a foreordained plan. He has chosen, rather, to share with humankind the task of crafting the events of each day, for he has placed himself in a position where he can be persuaded to, or dissuaded from, a course of action through prayer. God therefore invites us to participate with him in bringing the future into being. This means that while God has set in place eventual endpoints and goals that must be attained, he may not know the details of the future on a day-to-day basis.

In this view, God did not foresee the terrorist attack on the World Trade Center on 11 September 2001, and is therefore not culpable for allowing it. The attack was the terrifying price of humankind's refusal to live cooperatively in a bilateral relationship with God.

I don't believe that God can choose to be less than omnipotent and omniscient. The fact that he knows everything and stands outside of time doesn't change his ability to delight in us and interact with us as we journey through time. As such, I don't think open theism is convincing in its claim that God does not know the future. If scriptural passages exist which suggest that God is intimately and dynamically engaged with humankind, yet already knows the future, then we need a better theology that allows for both.

We are forced to conclude that open theism is not persuasive in letting God off the hook with regard to suffering.[12]

Is the hope of future glory justification enough for present suffering?

Is a theology that says that this universe is the best God could do an adequate one? Do we have to bear the consequences of God's pain-wracked initiative, comforted only by the fact that God has an eternal, pain-free life for us in the future?

In saying this, I don't want to downplay the hope that Christians have in God's future kingdom, a place where justice will finally come and every tear will be wiped dry (Revelation 21:1–5). It is highly probable that the obscenity of extreme suffering experienced now will dissolve into utter insignificance when seen against the glory of God's coming kingdom.

I also want to acknowledge that remaining faithful in our suffering (as Job did) honours God and is something that will be rewarded (Mark 10:29–30).

Be that as it may, the idea that this world of suffering is the best God can do right now leaves much to be desired. It is no comfort at all to the sole surviving member of a family killed by the natural evil of a tsunami, or to a Holocaust victim who has suffered from unspeakable moral evil.

To explore whether anything more can be said, we need to examine whether this world, and the way it has been set up, really is the best God can do.

Is this the best God can do?

Yes and no.

Yes in the sense that we are being blessed by God's best. In fact, the best is all that God can do. It must be clearly understood that God's plans are always perfect and that he is the final definition of good. As such, God's programme of preparing us for his eternal kingdom is solidly on track. No better plan exists and no better plan can be conceived. No Christ-honouring debate about suffering can allow that any of God's work is anything but perfect. Our task is not to put God on trial, but to understand those things that God allows us to understand so that we can be drawn into his plans – and ultimately rejoice in them.

With this important proviso, we can answer the above question by saying "No". God is able to create a world in which there are no tears. In fact, he has promised to do so. Scripture teaches that God will bring this current, imperfect Earth to an end and will judge and destroy all evil. He will then combine a renewed Earth with a new heaven to make one eternal kingdom in which he will be with us.[13] God is perfectly able, therefore, to make an existence that is free of the sort of suffering against which we now rail.

But of course, this is not a fair comparison. While God is perfectly able, it may not be his perfect plan. The fact is, the world that currently exists operates with moral and relational constraints that are very different from their counterparts in the coming kingdom. A world of danger, evil, and suffering is a necessary backdrop for evil to be expressed, judged, and finally killed off. A world of danger, evil, and suffering is perhaps also a necessary backdrop for us to be able to choose freely whether or not to accept the love of a holy God. Our current universe and God's coming kingdom have very different divine parameters. In this world, we are deciding *whether* to let Jesus be our Lord, while in God's coming kingdom, we will be exploring *how* we can celebrate Jesus as our Lord.

Even if we accept this… there is still a niggling concern that asks: Why is there so much apparently unnecessary suffering from natural causes? Is there a better understanding of God's good plan, a plan that permits suffering in this life? Can we do more than simply trot out the bland empiricism of science? Are we able to understand more if we allow an authentic synergy between the two disciplines of science and faith?

Understanding the first three chapters of Genesis

If we are to get into the theology of pain and suffering, we must consider the theological significance and principles taught by the Adam and Eve story – the account of human rebellion against God, and its consequences (an event referred to as "the fall").

Before we do this, it is worth noting that this account is placed at the very start of the Bible – and this is no accident. It represents the eternal principles that are foundational to the rest of Scripture. In other words, if these principles (written in a language understandable to all people) are not understood, then there is little point in reading further.

Christians are divided over how literally one should understand this story. But the truths that it teaches, about which most Christians agree are these:

- God freely chose to create us (and the universe we inhabit) in order to embrace us with his love.

- God risked giving us free will to accept or reject his love and lordship. He did so to win our freely chosen love.

- Humanity has largely chosen to reject God. The consequence of this is that suffering and death came into being, impacting humankind and all of creation.

Genesis 3 therefore invites us to take seriously the fact that something was lost and spoiled because of humanity's rejection of God's love and lordship. That rejection resulted in both physical evil (earthquakes and tsunamis) and moral evil (Hitler, Pol Pot, and perpetrators of cruel and abusive behaviour).

When God said that his creation was "good", what did he mean?

It is worth looking at how utopian any Edenic existence would have been. What is meant by it? Was it an idealistic, carefree existence, or was it a place where some suffering was allowed to mature us? Did God allow hunger to motivate us to be stewards of his creation responsible for making unproductive land productive (Genesis 1:28–29; 2:15)? Was it only later, when the wheels came off God's best plan for us as a result of our disobedience, that this work became onerous (Genesis 3:17–19)?

Or, was it the case that when God described his creation as "*good*" (Genesis 1:3–31), he didn't mean that it excluded suffering? Maybe it was good because it was an act of creation that fulfilled God's purposes? Could God therefore have allowed the existence of painful things right from the start – for good reason?

This is unlikely. We can't push this very far without fracturing the need to take seriously the fact that something was spoiled as a result of humankind's rebellion against God. We can't consider that our current universe is the final definition of "good" that God intended without challenging the teaching of Romans 8:22–23, which says that all of nature, as well as humankind, is waiting to be renewed.

Nevertheless, it is interesting to ponder whether there could have been some physical suffering before the fall. Would people have been protected from physical evil in Eden?

Logic suggests not. If sharp objects did not hurt, if fire did not burn, the result would have been chaotic. If unpleasant consequences did not mature us, we would be less than human.

So, if some suffering existed in humanity's pre-fallen state, what is the cut-off point between necessary Edenic pain and the horrible suffering that is the consequence of our choice to rebel against God?

Or is this irrelevant because the Eden scene is a metaphor rather than reality? If theologians are so silly with their Edenic machinations and imaginings about things that are metaphor, is it any wonder that theology is banished from science/faith conferences like an embarrassing child at a social gathering of sensible adults?

So, what do the opening chapters of Genesis have to say to us? Do they just leave us with a lot of unanswered questions that Christians bicker about interminably?

There does seem to be a logical disconnect between:

• the spoiling of an Edenic existence by the sin of humankind so that both nature and humanity wait for God's redemption (Romans 8:22–23)

and

- scientific evidence that an imperfect world existed well before humanoids came into being.

Both are credible, but at present they seem to be irreconcilable. These questions invite us to look deeper.

Let's do so. Let's dare to work at uncovering something more helpful than that which currently exists.

A theory

I want to propose a theory about suffering that joins the teaching of Genesis 3 and Romans 8 to the rationalism of Collins and Polkinghorne. It has, as its basis, the following three convictions:

1. God exists outside of time.
2. Suffering, extinctions, and predation occurred before the existence of humankind – before sin could ruin any Edenic existence.
3. Sin is an offence against God... and will ultimately be judged and destroyed by him.

If we take seriously the fact that something of God's ideal plan for us in this life was spoiled by the sin of humanity, we must ask: Why did dinosaurs get osteoarthritis?[14] Why did suffering exist before humans were around to ruin things? Was the horrible suffering that existed before humanity the "good" that God wanted (expressed in Genesis 1:3–31), or was it also the product of something imperfect and spoiled?

An examination of God's character as taught in Scripture would indicate the latter. Creation, through all of time, seems to be a good thing spoiled. But how can we allow for this theologically? Is there a model of thinking that might explain why dinosaurs got osteoarthritis?

Here's my thesis.

As God stands outside of time, an offence against God by humanity at any point in time can have implications for *all* of time. In other words, a judgment on sin can go backwards in time as well as forwards. Just as the death of Jesus was retrospective in paying for all sins committed by humankind before Calvary, so human sin was also retrospective in its consequences for the universe.

What, then, does this mean for the sequence found in the Genesis 1–3 narrative? Here we read that God created all things in a state of goodness, *then* human beings sinned against God, *then* God cursed creation, *then* suffering and death entered into creation.

The answer is surely that we are to understand "first" things in the creation sequence of Genesis as primal, foremost, normative – the way things were intended to be, are still intended to be, and indeed will be. They are not to be understood literally in the sense of "earliest" or "initial".

And so we have a model of suffering that fuses biblical principles with science. Because God stands outside of time, sin against God brings a consequence that affects all of time. The curse of sin goes backwards and forwards in history – just as the implications of Jesus' death on the cross go backwards and forwards in history.

This understanding means that:

- Dinosaurs can get osteoarthritis.
- Wasteful, primitive mass extinctions can occur.
- Human sin remains a reality.

- The need for both nature and humanity to be renewed remains intact (Romans 8:22–23).
- The hope of God's coming kingdom continues to motivate.
- The principles of Genesis remain in place.
- The scientific reality of a dangerous, creative, self-complexifying universe is maintained.

This, I submit, is consistent with biblical principles and with scientific understanding.

Father, Son, and Holy Spirit… and suffering

A beautiful and comprehensive answer to the subject of suffering can be gleaned from the Bible's teaching on the triune nature of God (Father, Son, and Holy Spirit).

When we cried out against God in our suffering and despaired of there ever being a final solution, God introduced himself to us as the *Father* who will have the last word. With the certainty of one who stands outside of time, the Father has set a date when this present age will be replaced by a new order uncorrupted by sin and suffering.

When we cried out against God that he did not understand how it feels to be a victim of suffering, God introduced himself to us as the *Son* – one who has experienced the agonies of life personally, and so understands what we go through.

When we cried out against God because all we could do when confronted by suffering was look on helplessly, God introduced himself to us as the *Holy Spirit* – his very own empowering presence. The Holy Spirit who comes to live within us compels us to address suffering practically wherever we come across it.

So, while bad things happen to good people, God sees to it that good people happen to bad things.

God's promises

God promises in his word that, while it may not be possible to remove suffering now, he will always be present with us to help us through it. Not only that, but he will never allow his authority in any situation to be entirely absent.

The Christian conviction is that even if God has not yet chosen to bring about complete victory over our suffering now, there will come a time when he will establish his new kingdom… and our victory over suffering will be complete. The final book of the Bible says that God will "*wipe away every tear from their eyes. There will be no more death or mourning or crying or pain, for the old order of things has passed away*" (Revelation 21:4). If we view suffering from the perspective of God's eternal kingdom, its ability to have the final word is destroyed.

And so we arrive at this conclusion: The only truly satisfying answer to the obscenity of suffering is eternity with God. Anything else is unsatisfactory, as it allows injustice to win.

Understand all the facets of suffering

To fully appreciate a beautiful diamond, it is necessary to understand all of its facets. The same is true of suffering. If we are to have a comprehensive and balanced understanding of what the Bible teaches about suffering, we must appreciate all of its facets. Here's a summary of the main ones:

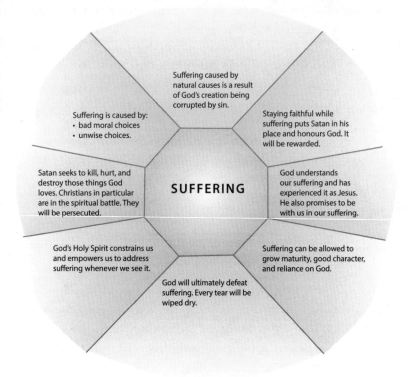

Suffering caused by natural causes is a result of God's creation being corrupted by sin.

Suffering is caused by:
• bad moral choices
• unwise choices.

Staying faithful while suffering puts Satan in his place and honours God. It will be rewarded.

Satan seeks to kill, hurt, and destroy those things God loves. Christians in particular are in the spiritual battle. They will be persecuted.

SUFFERING

God understands our suffering and has experienced it as Jesus. He also promises to be with us in our suffering.

God's Holy Spirit constrains us and empowers us to address suffering whenever we see it.

Suffering can be allowed to grow maturity, good character, and reliance on God.

God will ultimately defeat suffering. Every tear will be wiped dry.

How did God do?

God must always be more than we can conceive. As such, there will always be some mystery concerning him and his actions, particularly with regard to suffering. This should keep us humble and serve as a reminder to be careful with the claims we make.

Having said this, the fact remains that God has allowed us to understand a great deal. The teaching given in the Bible is extraordinarily balanced and comprehensive, giving real insight into all aspects of suffering. No part of it is silly or simplistic. In fact, it engenders a level of hope that is extraordinary.

The question is: Have you found God in this teaching? Has it surprised you and impressed you?

No other philosophy or religion that I have encountered offers such a satisfactory and comprehensive answer to the vexing subject of suffering.

The man in the pit

Do you remember the man who had fallen into the pit? Let me tell you the ending of the story:

> *After the last of the others had left, Jesus came to the edge of the pit. He saw the man at the bottom, climbed down into the pit, and lifted the man out.*

He will do the same for you.

4

THE EVIDENCE OF GOD IN MATHEMATICS

May I say quickly: this chapter is not a horrendous treatise on mathematics. I've written it simply to invite you to say "Wow!"

I'm actually not very good at maths. My fragile self-esteem in childhood meant that I'd go into a blue funk when taking a maths exam and become tormented by anxiety and humiliation. And yet, even in my school days, I thought mathematics was clever, almost magical, in what it could do.

Nothing has caused me to change that view since. By dint of a twelve-year career in biological research, I learned to bumble my way around statistics and was grateful for the rewards it gave me. The things that maths was able to reveal were remarkable.

Something wonderful seems to happen when the order of creation meets the intellect of human beings. Both are extraordinary... but together, they can do truly amazing things. We find ourselves able to describe the workings of the universe with mathematical equations that are beautiful. It seems that cosmic order sits there waiting for us to discover it and describe it.

Mathematics not only provides us with a language we can use to quantify what we see, but it also provides us with a path down which we can go and experience surprises along the way. It can reveal order and patterns in places we never expected to find them – as we shall discover later.

But to understand this, we needed to develop a mathematical language that was able to describe the order around us. This developed gradually over time as the need for more sophisticated mathematical expressions, such as "Sigma notation", arose. To use the analogy of music: it was as if we could hear the symphony, but it took time to devise a system that enabled us to write down the music we heard. The intriguing thing was, as we learned to codify the music, we discovered we could hear even more of it.

This leads to a question: Where does the music of mathematical patterns come from? Is it simply a product of human ordering, or is it something that exists independently of humankind?

People who ponder these sorts of things reside in the faculty of mathematical philosophy. You'd be amazed at how many of the world's most prestigious universities devote serious resources to the subject. It is a discipline with an inordinate love of "isms": Platonism, empiricism, logicism, formalism, conventionalism, psychologism, intuitionism, structuralism, fictionalism, nominalism – to name but a few.

One of the extraordinary qualities of maths is that it is not only a handy language for making sense of what exists, but it also enables us to conceptualize things that haven't yet been found. The Higgs boson is one such example – now happily confirmed as existing thanks to the Large Hadron Collider at CERN, near Geneva. Another example is the discovery of promethium in the Sun's atmosphere. It was found, despite never having being discovered on Earth. People looked for it because its existence fitted the mathematical pattern that the Russian chemist Dmitri Mendeleev observed in the periodic table.

Mathematics not only allows us to predict discoveries; it allows us to uncover things that we didn't even suspect were there. The Mandelbrot set is one such example. Let me tell you about it.

The mathematical surprises of the Mandelbrot set

Mathematicians have been staggered by the fact that equations that might reasonably be expected to draw chaotic pictures can actually produce beautiful, symmetrical, organic-looking patterns, which have the additional property of being infinitely magnifiable. In other words, these pictures behave as fractals. (A fractal is an entity that is the same regardless of scale – for example: tree trunks divide into limbs, which divide into branches, which divide into twigs.)

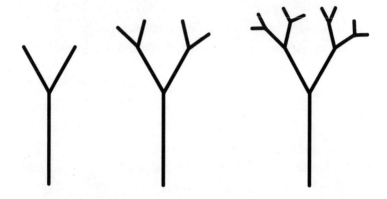

The Mandelbrot set is a fractal. It was named after the person who discovered it: the Polish-American mathematician Benoit Mandelbrot. The Mandelbrot set defines the boundary of a simple mathematical procedure derived from an innocuous looking equation. However, it turns out that the boundary of this set is infinitely complicated. Let me explain.

The Mandelbrot set

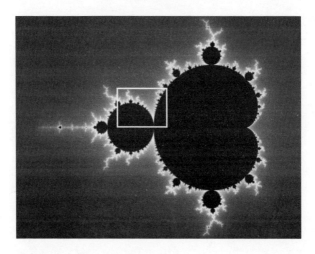

The Mandelbrot set acts as a fractal. It is infinitely magnifiable, being limited only by the power of the computer generating the set. If we zoom in to the section within the white-edged box in the middle, this is what we see:

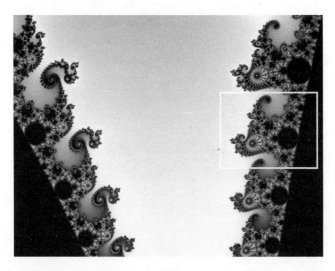

If we zoom into the section within the box again, this is what we see:

If we zoom into the section within the box again, this is what we see:

If we zoom into the section within the box again, this is what we see:

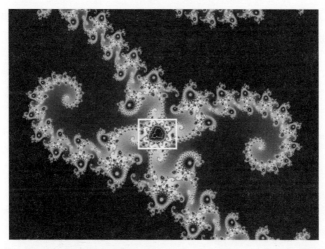

If we zoom into the section within the box again, this is what we see:

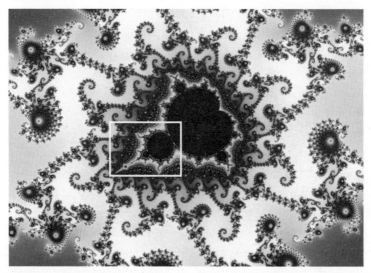

Did you notice the recurring theme of the original shape of the Mandelbrot?

Mathematics is a wonderful conceptual framework that is capable of surprising us with patterns in unexpected places.

Order is the scandal of the universe

There is an inherent purity to mathematics. It isn't messy like biology;[1] it is able to point clearly and unambiguously to the order that exists in the universe. Quite simply, *order* is the big surprise of the universe.

The question is: Where did this order come from? Could it have come from God?

God likes maths

God likes mathematics. That, at least, would be a fair verdict to arrive at if you looked at human history. It is significant that almost all philosophers up until Nietzsche were theists; certainly, the classical ones were.[2] Philosophy and mathematics have often walked hand in hand. Pythagoras, Plato, Galileo, Descartes, Pascal, Spinoza, Newton, Leibniz, and Laplace were all philosopher-mathematicians. It is alleged that Plato had "*Let no one ignorant of geometry enter*" engraved above the door of the academy he founded in Athens.

So, the shadow of God has fallen over mathematics for a goodly part of human history. The one discipline seems to have invited comment from the other. This has resulted in a zillion theories about what mathematics actually is.

Philosophers wonder whether maths is simply a language we have formulated to describe the order around us.

Partly, it is, but not entirely. As we have seen, maths can lead us to discoveries we didn't expect to make – for example, the Mandelbrot set.

Does maths therefore exist independently of humanity? Does

it sit there waiting for humanity to discover it like some hitherto unexplored land?

Partly, but not entirely. Maths doesn't really exist until we give it a voice (learn to notate it)… and so the debate continues on even today, resulting in many of the mathematical philosophy "isms" already alluded to. Tweaking these "isms" here and there has been particularly fertile ground for students seeking a PhD.

Most mathematical philosophers are realists. "Mathematical realism" holds that mathematical entities exist independently of the human mind. Humans don't invent mathematics; rather, they discover it. Triangles, for example, are real entities, not just creations of the human mind. However, they are perceived by the mind. The twentieth-century Austrian-born mathematician Kurt Gödel believed that objective mathematical reality could be perceived in a manner analogous to sense perception.

However, there is a problem with mathematical realism. It is this: Where and how do the mathematical entities exist, and how do we know about them? Is there a world, completely separate from our physical one, that is occupied by mathematical entities? On the one hand, mathematical truths seem to have a compelling inevitability, but on the other hand, the source of their truthfulness remains elusive.

How do we unify these different aspects of mathematics? How do we allow for the order of mathematics, its surprises, its mysteries, its comprehensibility, and its capacity to be codified into a language that can be beautiful?

We have arrived at the situation of a king who watches five blind men describe an elephant. One grabs the elephant's trunk and says the elephant is like a snake. Another grabs a tusk and says the elephant is like a horn. Yet another grabs a leg and says the elephant is like a tree trunk… and so on. Is there something that will enable us to make sense of the *whole* of mathematics – that will enable us to see all of the elephant, like the king?

Help from a surprising quarter: quantum physics

I believe a breakthrough in understanding the essence of what mathematics is (and does) can come from quantum physics.

Quantum physics examines the world of tiny, subatomic particles (smaller than an atom). It explores how these particles behave and what their relationship is to energy. In the quantum world, a particle can act as a wave or as a particle – sometimes both at the same time! The quantum world is really quite bizarre. It is a world in which particles can appear and disappear, or change their form depending on whether or not they are observed. The discovery of these phenomena in the last century caused a seismic shift in how we think about physics. It required scientists to move beyond having a purely mechanistic view of the material world and to consider matter in a completely different way. As a result, scientists no longer talk about electrons orbiting the nucleus of an atom. They talk about a "probability wave", which denotes where an electron *probably* is at any one time. Elementary particles are no longer *things*. Elementary particles define worlds of probabilities – not actualities. (This, incidentally, has given rise to speculation that subatomic particles could potentially inhabit different worlds!)

One of the scientists who pioneered the work of quantum physics was Werner Heisenberg. He became well known for the "uncertainty principle", which he developed in 1925. The Heisenberg uncertainly principle states that you can either know the velocity of an electron, or you can know its position, but you can't know both. This is just one of many paradoxes in the quantum world that physicists have learned to live with.

Heisenberg's work was developed further by the English

physicist Paul Dirac and the German physicist Erwin Schrödinger. As a result of their research, physicists have discovered that subatomic particles only appear when we actually observe them. It is the process of observation that results in them collapsing into physical reality. Professor Keith Ward likens this to how we see colour – for example, the colour of a yellow flower.[3] The colour doesn't exist of itself. It only exists when the reflected electromagnetic waves from the flower enter the rods and cones in the retina of our eyes… which results in electrical impulses travelling along nerves to our brain… which interprets the impulses as yellow.

It would seem that we live in a world of appearances. Things only exist when we observe them. Let me stress: this is not a lunatic, crackpot idea. This is serious science. Keith Ward reports the following comments by Nobel Prize-winning physicists:[4]

- The American physicist John Wheeler says: "No elementary phenomenon is real unless it is observed."

- The French physicist Bernard d'Espagnat says: "Physical reality is unknowable."

- The Hungarian-American physicist Eugene Wigner says: "Study of the external world leads to the conclusion that contents of consciousness are the ultimate reality."

- The Hungarian-American Nobel Prize-winning mathematical physicist John von Neumann says: "All real things are contents of consciousness."

Not all quantum physicists agree with these scientists, but many (with and without faith) do. They believe quantum physics indicates that consciousness lies behind the existence of all physical things.

You may well be wondering what the relevance of this is to mathematics. I was pondering this question (while cleaning my teeth prior to bed, actually), when I suddenly realized that the principles of quantum physics might solve the philosophical puzzle of what mathematics is.

Here's my thesis: Just as subatomic particles in the quantum world exist only when they are observed, so mathematics exists only when *it* is observed. And... just as consciousness is being discovered to be foundational to quantum physics, so consciousness is foundational to mathematics.

So, there it is, pure and simple.

Don't underestimate your toothbrush!

Let me reiterate: If consciousness lies behind the existence of all real things, and if mathematics is real and not just a concept, then it follows that mathematics must also be a "content of consciousness". It too must only exist because of consciousness.

This could solve the wrangle over what mathematics actually is. If we allowed our understanding of mathematics to be informed by quantum physics, we would see that it is quite possible that mathematics presents itself because of consciousness. Quantum physics would also allow mathematics to spring surprises... and yet be constrained within a rational discipline.

Could it be, then, that quantum physics allows us to view the whole elephant in company with the king?

The intriguing thing is this: the idea of underlying consciousness (or rationality) is entirely consistent with the idea of God.

A requiem for materialistic reductionism

The idea that everything can be explained from the bottom up by our atoms, chemical composition, and neural pathways has been blown out of the water by quantum physics. This may not have percolated through to the biological world of Richard Dawkins, but it will.

Not only is quantum physics a problem for Dawkins's materialistic reductionism but mathematical philosophy is as well. This is because the truths of mathematics are absolutely necessary – the human mind can establish why they must be so. The thing is, as the Australian mathematician James Franklin says, it is *"very difficult to explain how a purely physical brain could do that"*.[5]

So what does all this mean?

It means that the old deterministic way of thinking about reality – that we are all just the product of a lot of tiny billiard balls that bump into each other to create sentient beings – now has very little credence.

I hope that delights you. It certainly should add significance to your sense of being.

Science has journeyed a long way from Isaac Newton's mechanistic view of physics. Einstein was probably to blame for heralding this new wave of thinking. His famous equation, $E=mc^2$, showed that matter was simply a state of energy. If that were not strange enough, quantum physics suggests that matter may be even stranger – a "content of consciousness". The Danish physicist Niels Bohr says that those who are not shocked when they first come across quantum physics cannot possibly have understood it.[6] The American physicist Richard Feynman agrees. He says, *"I think I can safely say that nobody understands quantum mechanics."*[7]

Having said that, it should be stressed that quantum physics is not just a speculative philosophy; it is a highly predictive discipline. Physicists may not understand it, but they have found that maths works in concrete ways to give very useful, practical outcomes.

So, what can we conclude?

In the strange world of quantum physics, electrons can behave as either waves or particles – depending on whether or not they are observed. This means that scientists have to live with paradox, or as they call it, "complementarity". Quantum physics teaches us that electrons should, as we have said, more rightly be considered as "probability waves". Only at the point of experimental observation does a probability wave actually collapse into something. To put it another way, a "content of consciousness" is required to collapse a probability wave into something.

Other theories have been put forward to explain this phenomenon and more work is required. Nonetheless, there are good reasons to believe that physics is about consciousness. If so, the old, deterministic idea that matter gives rise to mind has been turned on its head. It may now be that mind gives rise to matter!

By equating matter to energy, Einstein began to dethrone matter as a fundamental reality. Quantum physics has completed the job. The intriguing thing is: this has always been known by theologians. They have understood for a very long time that we exist only because of the mind of God.

Enjoy this

You've earned a break from philosophy and quantum physics. Sit back and enjoy what follows. I've included it simply to show that mathematics can be beautiful. This, of course, doesn't prove God;

it is just another window into the order that we see in reality. The patterns in mathematics are just one of the many ways in which the universe shows evidence of mind.

$$1 \times 8 + 1 = 9$$
$$12 \times 8 + 1 = 98$$
$$123 \times 8 + 1 = 987$$
$$1234 \times 8 + 1 = 9876$$
$$12345 \times 8 + 1 = 98765$$
$$123456 \times 8 + 1 = 987654$$
$$1234567 \times 8 + 1 = 9876543$$
$$12345678 \times 8 + 1 = 98765432$$
$$123456789 \times 8 + 1 = 987654321$$

$$1 \times 9 + 2 = 11$$
$$12 \times 9 + 3 = 111$$
$$123 \times 9 + 4 = 1111$$
$$1234 \times 9 + 5 = 11111$$
$$12345 \times 9 + 6 = 111111$$
$$123456 \times 9 + 7 = 1111111$$
$$1234567 \times 9 + 8 = 11111111$$
$$12345678 \times 9 + 9 = 111111111$$
$$123456789 \times 9 + 2 = 1111111111$$

$$9 \times 9 + 7 = 88$$
$$98 \times 9 + 6 = 888$$
$$987 \times 9 + 5 = 8888$$
$$9876 \times 9 + 4 = 88888$$
$$98765 \times 9 + 3 = 888888$$
$$987654 \times 9 + 2 = 8888888$$
$$9876543 \times 9 + 1 = 88888888$$
$$98765432 \times 9 + 0 = 888888888$$

$$1 \times 1 = 1$$
$$11 \times 11 = 121$$
$$111 \times 111 = 12321$$
$$1111 \times 1111 = 1234321$$
$$11111 \times 11111 = 123454321$$
$$111111 \times 111111 = 12345654321$$
$$1111111 \times 1111111 = 1234567654321$$
$$11111111 \times 11111111 = 123456787654321$$
$$111111111 \times 111111111 = 12345678987654321$$

These beautiful patterns exist with the base 10 number system that we are used to. Of course, the convention of using ten numbers in maths (0–9) is, in a sense, arbitrary. (The Australian Aborigines, for example, use a base 5 numbering system.) Beautiful patterns that are more significant to mathematicians include this one: if you add consecutive odd numbers together, they make a perfect square.

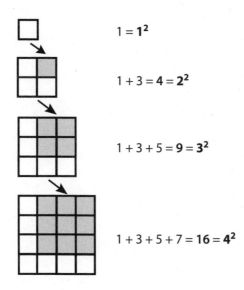

$$1 = 1^2$$

$$1 + 3 = 4 = 2^2$$

$$1 + 3 + 5 = 9 = 3^2$$

$$1 + 3 + 5 + 7 = 16 = 4^2$$

… and on and on, so that you get 5^2, 6^2, 7^2, 8^2, etc. all by adding consecutive odd numbers together.

Mathematicians get excited about this, honest!

Finally, here's another one they enjoy:

$(1 + 2 + 3 + 4 + 5 + 6 + 7 + 8 + 9 + 10)^2$ adds up to the same value as

$1^3 + 2^3 + 3^3 + 4^3 + 5^3 + 6^3 + 7^3 + 8^3 + 9^3 + 10^3$.

Everything is connected

Playing with mathematics has helped us to discover and define what we now call "chaos theory".

It all began when quantum physicists discovered some very "spooky" things. As we said earlier, scientists were discovering that subatomic particles could appear, disappear… and be in two places at the same time. Albert Einstein didn't like it. In 1935 he and his two colleagues, Boris Podolsky and Nathan Rosen, developed a "thought experiment" to demonstrate the inadequacy of quantum mechanics. (It was named the EPR experiment after the initials of each of their surnames.) The experiment showed that once two electrons interact with each other, they possess the power to influence each other no matter how far they separate. Even if one of the electrons flies off beyond the Moon, they have an intrinsic interconnectedness that cannot be broken. They are "entangled".[8] What you do to one particle is instantly mirrored in the other.

Einstein didn't like the idea, as it suggested that information from one particle could travel faster than the speed of light to the other – which was theoretically impossible. He referred to it as "spooky action at a distance".

Subsequent experiments, however, indicated that the spooky actions of EPR did actually occur. No one knows how or why.

The level of interconnectedness that exists in the universe frees it from slavishly following a predictable mechanistic path to an inevitable end. It allows genuine novelty. This is because the systems that exist in the universe are so exquisitely sensitive to circumstances that the slightest disturbance will make them behave in a totally different way.[9] The tiniest change in an initial condition of a system can result in a completely different outcome.

Take, for example, an air molecule that typically bumps into other such molecules fifty times in one ten thousandth of a second. It would be impossible to predict the direction of the final bounce if we did not take into account the gravitational attraction of a single electron on the other side of the observable universe. This is what one means by exquisite sensitivity.[10] This phenomenon has come to be known as "chaos theory".[11]

Chaos theory says that in some systems, small changes in initial conditions can lead to predictions so different that prediction itself becomes useless. The origins of the theory were developed in 1896 when the French mathematician Jacques Hadamard (1865–1963) proved that unless the initial conditions were perfectly defined, it was impossible to predict what three billiard balls would do when they careened off each other.

This inability to predict outcomes unless initial states were perfectly defined had been highlighted in 1887 when Oscar II, King of Sweden and Norway, offered a prize for the solution to the problem of whether or not the solar system was stable. The French mathematician Henri Poincaré (1854–1912) submitted his solution and won the prize, but a colleague discovered an error in his calculations. Poincaré was given six months to correct his proof in order to keep his prize, but he found that there was no solution. Predictions about the Earth, Moon, and Sun were impossible because small differences in the initial conditions produced greatly differing results. As such, the situation defied prediction.

In proving this, Poincaré effectively challenged the concept of a purely deterministic and predictable universe – an understanding that had been accepted since Sir Isaac Newton's law of universal gravitation led to the idea of a "clockwork universe".[12] This philosophy was developed by the eighteenth-century French mathematician Laplace, who said that God made the universe like a giant clock that had to work as it did.

In 1963, Edward Lorenz used Poincaré's mathematics to describe a simple mathematical model of a weather system.[13] The results were surprising in that his supposedly simple equations showed complex behaviour. He also discovered that the predicted behaviour of a system being modelled was highly sensitive to the initial conditions. This meant that without a very good understanding of the initial state of the system, it was impossible to predict the system's future. Lorenz said that such systems exhibited a "butterfly effect". This name came from his proposition that a butterfly stirring its wings over Hong Kong could initiate a chain of events that would affect the course of a tornado in Texas.[14]

It seems that even with a very good understanding of the initial state, some chaotic states are not predictable. They require us to factor in the tiniest of forces – which is often impossible. Everything in the cosmos appears to be extraordinarily connected.

Order is everywhere

Life for those studying chaos theory is made even more mystifying by the fact that some chaotic systems can behave in non-chaotic ways. If you plotted the successive events of a chaotic system on a three-dimensional graph, you would expect to end up with a chaotic mess. Often, you do. However, you sometimes end up with a beautiful pattern in which the sequence of events seems to circle around one particular point for a very long time. These favoured possibilities have been dubbed "strange attractors". In other words, there appears to be orderly disorder in some chaotic systems.[15] It's even possible for chaotic systems to have more than one strange attractor. Others don't seem to have any – or it might simply be that we haven't run the test long enough to find one.

If you want to entertain yourself, do an Internet search for visual representations of strange attractors – you will find some wonderful shapes.

The point of all this for us is simply that it's hard to find total chaos anywhere. It may even be impossible. The label "chaotic" may therefore be misleading.

The question is: Where does this order come from? Could it come from God?

Numbers that draw the universe

There are some remarkable numbers that seem to be able to draw the universe. One of them is the Fibonacci sequence, discovered by the twelfth-century Italian mathematician Leonardo Fibonacci (1170–1250). Fibonacci brought an idea from India to Europe that transformed Western mathematics. This idea was that the position of a number could determine its value. Take the number 125. The 1 in this number does not have a value of 1 but of 100 because of where it sits in the number.[16]

The mathematical sequence for which he is famous starts like this: 0, 1, 1, 2, 3, 5, 8, 13, 21, 34, 55 – and so on forever. Each number is the sum of the two numbers that precede it. It's a simple pattern, but it appears to be a numbering system that is built into the cosmos. The number of petals in a flower, for example, consistently follows the Fibonacci sequence.

The sequence is also seen in the microscopic realm. The DNA molecule is 34 angstrom long and 21 angstrom wide for each full cycle of its double helix spiral. These numbers – 34 and 21 – are numbers in the Fibonacci series, and their ratio is described as the "golden ratio".

The ratios of successive numbers of the Fibonacci sequence oscillate either side of the "golden ratio" – getting closer to it as the numbers get bigger. This golden ratio is represented by the Greek letter φ (phi) and its value is 1.618 – or, if you want to be strictly accurate, it is $(1 + \sqrt{5})/2$. This ratio crops up everywhere.

If you draw the diagonals on a pentagon, a golden ratio can be found wherever two lines of different length meet. For example, one golden ratio is that of a side to a diagonal.

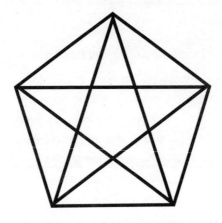

How many different pairs of lines forming golden ratios can you find? Can you find ten? Twenty? Thirty?

The golden ratio describes the two sides of a "golden rectangle", a shape that has been found to be particularly pleasing aesthetically. It crops up everywhere in art and architecture – for example, in the dimensions of the end face of the Parthenon in Athens. Leonardo da Vinci called this ratio the "divine proportion" and featured it in many of his paintings, including the *Mona Lisa*. If a rectangle is drawn that contains Mona Lisa's face, it will be found to be a golden rectangle. The rectangle can be divided again using her eyes as a horizontal divider.

The aesthetics of the golden rectangle have been exploited by the commercial world. You will even find it in some breakfast cereal boxes!

A golden
rectangle

Remove this square

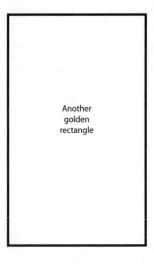

We can keep removing squares to form an infinite number of golden rectangles. If we join the corresponding corners of the squares with a curved line, it will draw a "golden spiral".

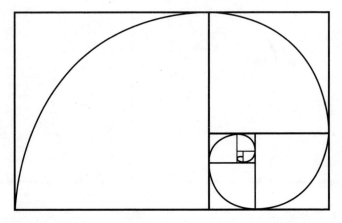

This golden spiral is a shape seen in seashells, spiral galaxies, and hurricanes.

Let's play some more. Take two adjacent sides of a golden rectangle...

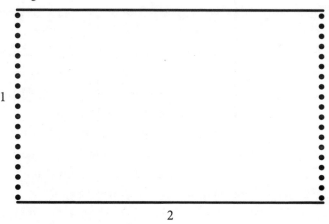

... and draw a circle with them.

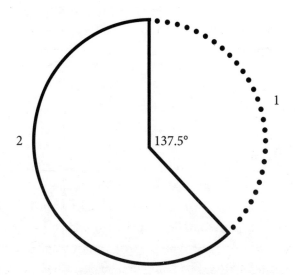

The angle subtended by the smaller arc is known as "the golden angle". It measures 137.5°.

It just so happens that there is a quantity in the theory of quantum electrodynamics called "the fine-structure constant". It's a fundamental constant of nature... and it has a value of about 1/137 (0.0073).

Nobody knows why this constant has this value. All that scientists are sure of is that it is a very important value. If the fine-structure constant were to change by just 4 per cent, stellar fusion inside stars would not produce carbon, and carbon-based life (which includes you and me) would not exist. Similarly, if it were greater than 0.1 (rather than the actual value of 0.0073), then stellar fusion would be impossible and no place in the universe would be warm enough for life to exist as we know it.[17]

It would seem that there are some very special numbers that help to define and draw the universe. Again, this is entirely consistent with the notion that there is a mind behind the universe – a mind that wanted stars to burn long enough to form the elements, which in turn allowed life to develop.

The mystery of why mathematics is so amazingly effective

On the border between France and Switzerland, there is a 27-kilometre circular tunnel that houses the Large Hadron Collider. It was built at a cost of 4.4 billion US dollars, and was designed primarily to find a sub-nuclear particle that was reasoned to exist on the basis of mathematics alone.

Now, I have to say, that's a big bet to make on a sum being right!

Fortunately, the sub-nuclear particle (dubbed by journalists "the God particle") was found. It was confirmed as existing on 14 March 2013, forty-nine years after Higgs and a bunch of other scientists reasoned from mathematics that it had to exist. The particle, the Higgs boson, was named in his honour.

All this points to the fact that mathematics is amazingly effective at describing and uncovering the fabric of the universe. The Hungarian-American physicist Eugene Wigner understood this and spoke of "*the unreasonable effectiveness of mathematics in the natural sciences*".[18]

It's worth asking why this is so.

Here's another story:

Quantum physics seeks to understand the world of subatomic particles such as an electron. Einstein's "special relativity", on the other hand, looks at very fast objects. The Cambridge physicist Paul Dirac was intrigued about what would happen when these two branches of physics were brought together and an electron was accelerated so that it went very fast. He worked out from mathematics that the only way the requirements of these two branches of physics could be resolved was if a totally new object existed, a positively charged mirror image of the electron. He called this theoretical particle a "positron". The positron was the "anti-matter" of an electron.

Four years later, the American physicist Carl Anderson discovered the positron by using a "cloud chamber".

The significant thing about all this is that a particle was discovered by mathematics before it was discovered in reality.

Paul Dirac later reflected on the power of mathematics and why it is that nature is constructed on such beautiful mathematical lines. He said: "*God is a mathematician of a very high order, and he used very advanced mathematics in constructing the universe.*"[19]

Why do we see such beauty in the complex mathematics of the universe? Why is mathematics so "unreasonably effective"? What does this indicate?

The philosopher and theologian Vern Poythress has explored the metaphysical nature of mathematics. He reminds us that the very notion that 2 + 2 = 4 is not something everyone agrees with. Vedantic Hinduism, for example, understands plurality to be an illusion. This highlights the fact that mathematics can only exist in a world that acknowledges plurality. Moreover, it can only exist in a universe that is ordered and constant. Two apples must remain two apples while they are being counted… and they must continue to be two apples tomorrow when they are counted again. The very dependability of mathematics reflects a world that is rational and comprehensible – a world that allows us to do science.[20]

Poythress describes mathematics as "*the rhyme of the universe*". By this he means that, just as rhyme is one part of a poem, so mathematics is one aspect of an ordered universe. And, like the rules of rhyme, mathematics is foundational of the whole. He goes on to say that mathematics embodies victory over chaos. It reflects an order that theism explains well.[21] Its very dependability reflects the faithful, unchanging nature of God.

He makes a good point.

Why can we understand the universe?

It may be a little unsettling, but the fact remains that a chimpanzee and a human being have 98.8 per cent of their DNA in common. We are very close cousins, biologically speaking – but we are vastly different. Only humans have the ability to reach for the stars and comprehend the cosmos. Through the agency of mathematics, with its beautiful equations, we have unlocked many of the secrets of the universe and discovered how it works – even to its furthest ends. It seems that we have been given the ability to do so, and perhaps even the invitation to do so.

Goldilocks and the magical hat called "infinity"

All science proceeds on the assumption that the universe is rational and intelligible – and mathematics codifies this rationality. As such, all scientists have faith. The mathematical physicist and cosmologist Paul Davies says scientists have to have faith "*that the universe is governed by dependable, immutable, absolute, universal, mathematical laws of an unspecified origin… [To] think that such laws exist without reason is anti-rational.*"[22]

The conundrum of where these laws come from cannot be swept under the carpet by postulating that our universe is just one of an infinite number of universes, each with its own unique set of physical laws. According to proponents of this theory, it was inevitable that one universe should eventually be the "Goldilocks Universe" – the one that was "just right" to allow sentient life to develop. But this, as Paul Davies points out, simply dodges the issue: "*There has to be a physical mechanism to make all those universes and bestow [scientific] bylaws on them. This process will require its own laws, or meta-laws. Where do they come from?*" He concludes that both religion and science are founded on faith – namely, on belief in the existence of something outside the universe. [23]

That's not a bad statement from a distinguished scientist with no conventional faith!

Let's talk about infinity.

As we have said, one of the ways some people have sought to explain the existence of a universe so finely tuned to allow life is to suggest that it would have to exist if there were an infinite number of universes. The theory is that our universe is just one in a giant multiverse complex. An infinite number of universes either exist concurrently or occur because one universe seeds another successively. It is suggested that physical laws governing the running of a universe come into being at the genesis of each universe. As such, physical laws are not trans-universal. They are, if you like, local bylaws specific for a particular universe. The argument goes on to suggest that because a multiverse of infinite size presents infinite possibilities, a universe such as ours would have to eventually come into existence and generate sentient life able to observe the universe around it purely by chance.

There are, however, many difficulties with this thinking.

In essence, it simply transcribes Fred Hoyle's discredited steady state universe (see Chapter 1) into a steady state multiverse. It does not solve the problem of where the initial conditions for a universe came from. It simply says they exist because they exist... which is lazy thinking.

The way some atheists appeal to infinity in order to explain everything should cause concern. There is a logical absurdity about them scorning Christians for putting their faith in "mindless superstition" to explain the universe when they put their faith in infinity to do the same thing.

On the basis of cause and effect, belief that the universe exists because of a higher mind makes a lot more sense than dipping a hand into a magical hat called "infinity", believing that it can produce everything. While there is good reason to believe that a mind is behind the order of the universe, there is no scientific basis for believing that infinity has the ability to produce anything. Infinity can never be a prime cause. It can only provide the chance for something to change – nothing more. It has no ability to initiate any creative act.

If atheists insist that cosmic infinity exists within the dimension of time, then they have failed to tell us where time began. This is a bit of an embarrassment, given that time only began when matter was created. Einstein discovered this, and in doing so, verified the same statement made by St Augustine of Hippo fourteen centuries earlier. (It must have been nice for theologians to see science catch up!)

Certainly, it is difficult to conceive how an infinity that allows a sequence of universes to come into being could exist outside of time. While clock-type time may not exist in a system that allows multiverses, sequential time (in which one act follows another) would have to exist if one universe has the ability to seed another.

If, however, atheists insist that cosmic infinity exists outside of time, then creative, eternal infinity has moved from being a mathematical concept to something that looks a lot like God.

Ouch!

Let me say it again: for atheists to accuse Christians of dipping their hand into the magical hat of theism in order to explain things when they are dipping their hand into the even more unlikely hat of infinity is to fracture common sense.

Why do we have the ability to unlock the secrets of the universe?

Many scientists are asking why humankind has the marvellous power to understand things. We alone have the ability to unlock the secrets of the universe. The particle physicist and theologian John Polkinghorne marvels that the universe is so astonishingly open to us and is rationally transparent to our enquiry. In his view, the fact that we understand the subatomic world of quantum theory and the cosmic implications of general relativity goes far beyond anything that could conceivably be of relevance to survival fitness.[24]

Our universe is extraordinarily intelligible to us, and it allows mathematics to unlock its secrets. This remarkable feature requires an explanation. Polkinghorne suggests that theism provides just such an explanation. "*If the universe is the creation of a rational God, and we are creatures made in the divine image, then it is entirely logical that there is order in the universe and that it is accessible to our minds.*"[25]

Some scientists have wondered not only why the universe is intelligible, but why the mathematical equations that explain the laws of physics are themselves beautiful. Paul Dirac (1902–84), a physicist at Cambridge University, says that it is more important that there be beauty in scientific equations than that they should be right, because if they were ugly, there is no chance that they could be right.[26]

The philosopher and mathematician Bertrand Russell voices a similar sentiment regarding pure mathematics:

> *Mathematics, rightly viewed, possesses not only truth, but supreme beauty… sublimely pure, and capable of a stern perfection such as only the greatest art can show. The true spirit of delight, the exaltation, the sense of being more than Man, which is the touchstone of the highest excellence, is to be found in mathematics as surely as poetry.*[27]

It seems that there is something in the language of mathematics that reflects the qualities of God and helps us uncover the mind of God. It is not a knockout blow – a proof of God – for it is not the nature of God to employ any *tour de force* to compel faith. Rather, it is a simple invitation, written with truth and reason, that invites faith.

5

THE EVIDENCE OF GOD IN SOCIETY

Stephen ruffled the hair of my eleven-year-old son, Michael, and said he would kill him if he let in a goal. Michael was goalkeeper in a soccer match that was being played on asphalt near the docklands of Kowloon, opposite Hong Kong. The fact that this soccer match was occurring at the same time as a basketball match was being played across its width did not seem to bother anyone. Space was at a premium.

I smiled, knowing that Michael was about as safe from murder as he would ever be in his life. This was perhaps surprising, given that Stephen had been a member of a particularly violent Triad society from China. If that were not bad enough, many members of his soccer team had once been members of the 14K Triad society, which ruled the less salubrious areas of Kowloon and Hong Kong with its own particular brand of viciousness.

The one thing that made the difference was that these young men – who had once lived lives steeped in unimaginable violence and depravity – had become Christians. This had come about through the ministry of the Society of Stephen, an organization founded by Jackie Pullinger, a missionary who works among gang members, drug addicts, prostitutes, and street sleepers in the no-go areas of Hong Kong. Her love for God and sacrificial love for others is inspirational – and she is a dear friend.

There are millions of stories like this. One of the best known is that of John Newton (1725–1807). John Newton was a difficult young man who had been hardened by a life at sea and brutalized by a public flogging. He had seriously contemplated murdering the ship's captain who ordered his flogging and came to have little compunction about abusing others. Perhaps not surprisingly, he became a slaver. Ironically, he was later forced to become a slave himself to the African wife of a slave-master in West Africa. He was eventually rescued, and encountered God during a storm at sea as he returned to England.

After his conversion, Newton trained to become an Anglican priest. He worked in London as an evangelical minister and became an ally and friend of William Wilberforce, helping him to bring about the abolition of slavery in Britain. The fact that God could forgive Newton after all that he had done moved him to pen the words of the great hymn "Amazing Grace".

No religion in the world has transformed so many people as profoundly as authentic Christianity. This claim has been put well by the Eastern Orthodox theologian David Bentley Hart in a big juicy statement. He says:

> *Among all the many great transitions that have marked the evolution of Western civilization… there has been only one – the triumph of Christianity – that can be called in the fullest sense a "revolution": a truly massive and epochal revision of humanity's prevailing vision of reality, so pervasive in its influence and so vast in its consequences as to actually have created a new conception of the world, of history, of human nature, of time, and of the moral good.*[1]

It seems that God causes people to be good – and this has enormous implications for society.

The fact that God is good for society doesn't prove his existence, of course. But if Christianity is true, and Jesus shows us what God's character is like, then Christianity *has* to be good for society. So, let's ask whether this is the case. Is there any evidence of God to be found in society?

Here are a few stories to begin our thinking:

Some stories of revival

The Welsh Revival of 1904–1905 resulted in 150,000 people committing their lives to Christ. It was an extraordinary phenomenon. Several leaders played key roles in the revival, but one in particular was at its heart. His name was Evan Roberts. Evan came from the small town of Loughor near Swansea. He left school at the age of eleven to work with his father down in the coalmines. Evan used to take his Bible with him into the mine and read it during the rest periods. He left the mines in his mid-twenties to become an apprentice blacksmith to his uncle in nearby Pontarddulais. Evan had little education; he simply had a hunger for God and a willingness to obey him regardless of the cost. He prayed every day for thirteen years for revival to come to his native land.

Then it came.

As Evan spoke at meetings, inviting people to confess their sins and commit their lives to Jesus, people fell in love with God and their lives were transformed. Men stopped impoverishing their families by spending their money on drink; instead they began feeding and clothing them properly. Fractured family relationships were restored. The crime rate dropped to such an extent that the work of the police reduced markedly and the magistrates had little to do. Miners sang hymns down in the mines. The pit ponies hauling the coal carts had to learn to be cajoled into action by language that didn't include curses. Productivity and prosperity increased, particularly in the industrial towns of South Wales.

An extraordinary aspect of this revival was that it spread through Welsh communities throughout the world. For two years, it burned like a fire… and then, sadly, it began to fade. The fact that the revival was not a lasting phenomenon broke Evan Roberts' heart.

The symptoms of revival and its consequences for society have been consistent throughout history. They have certainly been seen in the recent revivals chronicled by George Otis Jr in his *Transformation* video series. Some of these have occurred in Cali, Columbia; Kiambu, Kenya; Hemet, California; and Almongonga, Guatemala. Although revivals can be short-lived, their effects linger on in the culture of communities and families for a long time.

While revivals seem to be a sovereign act of God, history indicates that God often brings them about in response to heartfelt prayers and tears. These tears are not something conjured up to attract the attention of an indifferent God; they are an expression of empathy with God at his grief over evil and injustice. People cry because evil is anti-God and unlike God. People cry because evil is wrong and so terribly destructive, particularly to the poor and vulnerable. People cry because God is holy and the hearts of those who are good ache for good.

America has experienced societal transformation as a result of revival on a number of occasions. The three or four waves of religious enthusiasm that occurred between the early eighteenth century and the late nineteenth century are known collectively as the "Great Awakening".

The first wave, in 1730–43, came in the form of frontier

revivals led by Jonathan Edwards and George Whitefield. The wave after that was headed by abolitionists and the temperance unions. Dwight L. Moody and his compatriots led yet another wave that resulted in magnificent work among the poor.

More recently, there was the charismatic renewal of the 1960s and 70s.

It is interesting to note that revivals generally happen outside the orbit of mainline Christian denominations. Perhaps the level of centralized power and control in these institutions stifles renewal. Certainly, the ministry of John Wesley was scorned by the Church of England. They did not approve of him crossing parish boundaries into areas for which local clerics felt they had exclusive responsibility. As a result, he was often forbidden from preaching in churches and compelled to operate out in the open. Given the size of the crowds that came to listen to him, this was perhaps propitious.

The leadership of the Church of England was suspicious both of Wesley's enthusiasm for God and of his habit of organizing local Christians into small groups (classes) to study God's word. They felt he was devolving the authority of Anglican clerics and putting it in the hands of lay preachers. When Wesley learned that most Church of England ministers had been recalled to England after the American War of Independence, he tried to persuade the Bishop of London to send ministers back to America. When this did not happen, Wesley ordained three of his preachers and sent them to America. This helped seal the rift between himself and the Church of England.

In my own country of Australia, revival came in 1979 to Galiwin'ku (Elcho Island) off the north coast. The minister of the island was Djiniyini Gondarra, an Aborigine from Arnhem Land who had been trained in the Methodist tradition. His work on Galiwin'ku hadn't borne much fruit and he was experiencing significant opposition from many in the local community. After returning from a two-month holiday, he met with some local people in his manse for prayer. While they prayed that night, the Holy Spirit fell on them in much the same way as it fell on Jesus' disciples at Pentecost. The meeting lasted all night. Many spoke of being healed and of being filled with God's Spirit.

The evangelist Dan Armstrong arrived six weeks later on what he called "the crest of the wave" to bring encouragement and add momentum to the renewal movement. People met and engaged in free-flowing, spontaneous worship for hours. They were hungry to learn about God.[2] Local church attendance increased more than tenfold in a few months.

The movement spread from Elcho to Aboriginal communities in the north, centre, and west of Australia. Wherever it went, it transformed people's health, education, and work ethic. In particular, it brought reconciliation to families, clans, and tribes that had been fighting each other for generations.

The Australian Aboriginal community has a good understanding of the transforming power of the Christian gospel. Yirara College was established in 1973 as a government residential college for Aboriginal students who came from isolated communities in central Australia. Its purpose was to expose Aboriginal youth to social development through educational programmes designed to help them adjust to Western society.

It did not work. The students and the college became severely dysfunctional. Government bureaucrats responded by consulting the Aboriginal people living in the isolated feeder communities of central Australia. The elders from these communities said they wanted Yirara to be a Christian school run by the Lutherans of Fink River Mission. When the Lutherans took over, the college was transformed. It brought spiritual and social reform that provided stability and hope.

It seems that wherever Christianity has been imposed in a way that is not Christ-like – that is to say, without love and understanding – the results have been disastrous. However, when Christianity has been applied in a Christ-like way, it has invariably been transformative, emancipatory, and hope-giving.

The real deal

In looking for the evidence of God in society, it is important to draw a distinction between authentic Christianity, involving faithful adherence to Jesus' teachings, actions, and lifestyle… and what is sometimes practised by religious institutions that are not always Christ-like. It is very difficult for institutions to escape being corrupted by a very unchristian addiction to power and status. Jesus' notions of sacrificial love – even for one's enemies – and of putting a priority on the wellbeing of others are not characteristics typically associated with powerful political institutions. As such, it would be unfair to consider anything other than the "real deal" in Christianity when searching for evidence of God in society.

Christianity is good for communism!

Communist China is not known for being kind to Christianity. Pastors of churches not belonging to the tightly controlled "Three-Self Patriotic Movement" often spend lengthy periods in prison. It was therefore something of a surprise to read that the owner of the Boteli Valve Group in Wenzhou, China, wanted to see all his staff convert to Christianity.[3] This factory is one of a number of businesses whose success is being studied by the Chinese government.

The Boteli Valve Group makes 5 million dollars' worth of valves every month, 40 per cent of which are exported. The factory's general manager, Weng-Jen Wau, says he wants all his workers to become Christians. Why? "*Because Christians make better workers.*" As such, a Christian culture is encouraged in the factory. Every Monday morning, the senior managers gather together and pray for the business.

Weng-Jen Wau says, "*If you're a Christian you're more honest, with a better heart.*" He also says that Christians are more responsible. "*When they do things wrong, they feel guilty – that's the difference.*"

Professor Zhuo Xinping, Director of the Chinese Institute of World Religions, says, "*I think if all enterprises absorb this Christian culture, we will have a much more harmonious society.*" He goes on to say that Chinese researchers are considering whether there is a link between economic prosperity and Protestant Christianity – and they are questioning what this might mean for today's China.

That's not a bad endorsement of Christianity's ability to transform industry in society! Interestingly, this idea was picked up by George Washington, who said:

> *We are persuaded that good Christians will always be good citizens, and that where righteousness prevails among individuals the Nation will be great and happy. Thus while just government protects all in their religious rights, true religion affords to government its surest support.*[4]

This is entirely consistent with the Apostle Paul's teaching in Romans 13:1–7, where he speaks of the need for Christians to be good citizens.

God is good for the land

Societies develop in the context of the land around them. As such, the prosperity of society is usually reflected in the prosperity of the land. It is therefore worth asking whether God is good for the land.

A search of the Scriptures is enlightening, for it shows that true godliness causes the land to prosper. Let me explain.

The Israelites have always thought of God as being active in history, particularly in their history. Their national identity was, and is, defined by their faith and the land God gave them to live in. Military activity in defence of their land was seen to be a defence of their faith.

Good productivity of the land and military success in defending it were seen as God's reward for faithfulness. Desolation and defeat were seen to be the result of unfaithfulness.

Care of the land and the wellbeing of the land were reflections of faithfulness to God. This was consistent with the teaching of Genesis, which says that God is responsible for the existence of everything. The environment and all that God made is described using the Hebrew word *towb*, meaning "good/pleasant/precious" (Genesis 1:4, 10, 12, 18, 21, 25, 31). In other words, the environment, and everything God has made, has inherent worth. God chose to make it and considered it all "good".

However, in giving us free will to choose between good and evil, evil was allowed the chance to hijack God's best plan for creation. As a consequence, pain, greed, and godlessness made their appearance. The rest of the story of the Bible is the unfolding of God's plan to rescue it all back.

Some people seem to think that because creation has gone to the dogs and will be replaced at some future date with God's eternal kingdom, it can be scorned, abused, and pillaged. The teaching of Romans 8:20–22, however, makes it clear that God's creation is waiting for the full realization of redemption, just like us. As such, we cannot abuse it any more than we can abuse each other. Far from it. We should prefigure the values of God's kingdom now – and value everything that God has made.

The Genesis story teaches that humankind is to subdue the environment and make it fruitful (Genesis 1:28). And we are to do that in much the same way a gardener would subdue an unruly garden. The Hebrew word *kbs*, meaning "subdue", can also mean "violate", but that is not its meaning in this context. We are stewards of God's property and so we are not to waste or despoil it. God commanded Adam and Eve to work the land and "*take care of it*" so that it was fruitful (Genesis 2:15).

I have seen an Australian Aborigine replace half of a clump of yam bulbs so that they could provide food in future seasons. I have also watched TV programmes that show the desert being irrigated and farmed. I'm sure that God smiles at both. God did not create the land to be empty. Leviticus 19:23–25 speaks of God commanding his people to plant fruit trees (and to maximize the harvest by not picking the fruit prematurely). The Old Testament Israelites believed that the bounty produced from the land was a gift from God (Deuteronomy 7:13).

It is interesting to note, in passing, that Genesis not only mentions the practical qualities of trees and plants but also their aesthetic qualities. "*The LORD God made all kinds of trees grow out of the ground – trees that were pleasing to the eye and good for food*" (Genesis 2:9). From the very start, it was God's intention that trees should adorn the world and make it beautiful. This is a lovely value to uphold, and one that has implications for the quality of life in human society.

Sadly, lack of understanding, short-term expediency, and greed have led us to desecrate this gift from God. Our high technology, high finance, and high-rises can too easily create the illusion that we are masters of our own destiny. Self-obsession that feels no obligation to God is called sin.

The Adam and Eve story teaches us that humankind's rebellion against God resulted in the land being cursed so that growing food would be a struggle (Genesis 3:17–19). It is important to note that our rebellion and our resultant battle with the land is not God's best will for us. It is a consequence of sin.

This set a consistent pattern in the history of Israel. The authors of the Old Testament wrote that whenever people sinned against God, it resulted in their land being unproductive. Sin defiled the land.

> *The earth dries up and withers, the world languishes and withers, the heavens languish with the earth. The earth is defiled by its people; they have disobeyed the laws, violated the statutes and broken the everlasting covenant. Therefore a curse consumes the earth; its people must bear their guilt.*
>
> (Isaiah 24:4–6)

> *I brought you into a fertile land to eat its fruit and rich produce. But you came and defiled my land and made my inheritance detestable.*
>
> (Jeremiah 2:7)

When the Old Testament spoke of sin "defiling the land", it was commenting on more than the people's morality. Rebellion against God really did, in the most literal sense, result in good land being laid waste:

*He [God] turned rivers into a desert, flowing springs
into thirsty ground, and fruitful land into a salt waste,
because of the wickedness of those who lived there.*

(Psalm 107:33–34)

*Why has the land been ruined and laid waste like a
desert that no one can cross? The LORD said, "It is
because they have forsaken my law…"*

(Jeremiah 9:12–13)

*Hear the word of the LORD, you Israelites, because
the LORD has a charge to bring against you who live
in the land: "There is no faithfulness, no love, no
acknowledgment of God in the land. There is only
cursing, lying and murder, stealing and adultery; they
break all bounds, and bloodshed follows bloodshed.
Because of this the land dries up, and all who live in it
waste away; the beasts of the field, the birds in the sky
and the fish in the sea are swept away."*

(Hosea 4:1–3)

This is never more true than today, when rebellion against God's principles still results in good land being laid waste. We see it clearly in nations where peace and civility have broken down.

The ancient Israelites thought that God was the agent of destruction. We might rather say today that God has organized things so that we suffer the consequences of our own ungodly actions in the desolation of the land that we despoil. In the final analysis, it is much the same.

Being careless of the land seems to go hand in hand with being careless of God: "*They will turn my pleasant field into a desolate wasteland. It will be made a wasteland, parched and desolate before me; the whole land will be laid waste because there is no one who cares"* (Jeremiah 12:10–13).

It is when we imagine that we will not answer to God for our ruinous selfish activities that environmental exploitation continues without restraint.

God, therefore, is good for the land... and that's good for society.

The confessions of an atheist

My church community is small. We worship in a primary school hall and we own next to nothing. It is, however, an extraordinary community. Although only about eighty people attend on any Sunday morning, we have ten groups meeting in people's homes. It is an intensely relational church. A small team works in the local housing estate of nearly a hundred flats. Many of those housed there are among the most disadvantaged people in Adelaide. Since the team started working there, the number of police call-outs to the estate has halved. This statistic is not reported by the media.

Our church operates its overseas mission arm through an organization called "Empart", which trains local church planters in Asia. Many of these pastors' homes become the local orphanage. Empart also teaches poor women the skill of sewing and gives them a sewing machine so they can earn a living. Our church gives sacrificially to this work and occasionally sends teams to India to help.

One of these teams went to the Indian state of Orissa just after a local uprising had occurred against Christians. Many local Christians had been killed by Hindu extremists. During the team's entire time in Orissa, they did not see one atheist worker seeking to help any of the 35,000 displaced Christians hiding in the jungles of Orissa. But the Christians were there. This was not reported by the media.

Christianity's ability to transform culture and give hope has been noted in Africa, even by atheists. Matthew Parris, a writer for *The Times* and former Member of Parliament in the UK, is not your typical atheist. He wrote an article on 27 December 2008, saying, "*As an atheist, I truly believe Africa needs God. Missionaries, not aid money, are the solution to Africa's biggest problem – the crushing passivity of the people's mindset.*"

After researching a story on aid organizations in Africa, Parris wrote:

> *Travelling in Malawi refreshed a belief I've been trying*
> *to banish all my life, but an observation I've been*
> *unable to avoid since my childhood. It confounds my*
> *ideological beliefs, refuses to fit my worldview and has*
> *embarrassed my growing belief that there is no God.*

He goes on to say:

> *I've become convinced of the enormous contribution*
> *that Christianity makes in Africa: sharply distinct from*
> *the work of secular and government organisations*
> *and international aid efforts. These alone will*
> *not do. Education and training alone will not do.*
> *Christianity changes people's hearts. It brings spiritual*
> *transformation.*

So, even atheists are discovering that no one is doing very well without Christianity. Without Jesus, Africa reverts to tribal warfare, abusive overlords, urban gangsterism, and militant Islam. Parris says that removing Christianity from Africa risks *"leaving the continent at the mercy of a malignant fusion of Nike, the witch doctor... and the machete".*

It is worth quoting from Mark Steyn, a columnist for the Canadian paper *Western Standard*. He wrote in his book, *America Alone*, *"There are no examples of sustained atheist civilizations. Atheistic humanism became inhumanism in the hands of the Fascists and Communists."*[5]

Nietzsche, nature, and Jonathan

The English rabbi and scholar Jonathan Sacks has written an explosive article entitled "Atheism has failed: Only religion can defeat the new barbarians". In it, he says, *"You cannot expect the foundations of western civilisation to crumble and leave the rest of the building intact."* He goes on to speak of the German atheist philosopher Friedrich Nietzsche. In Nietzsche's later writings, he warns that losing the Christian faith will mean abandoning Christian morality. This, as Sacks explains, leaves us in some very chilly waters: *"No more 'Love your neighbour as yourself'; instead, the 'will to power'. No more 'Thou shalt not'; instead, people would live by the law of nature, the strong dominating or eliminating the weak."*[6]

Sacks makes the point that the new atheists are both presumptuous and careless when talking about secular morality: *"If asked where we get our morality from, if not from science or religion, the new atheists start to stammer. They tend to argue that ethics is obvious, which it isn't..."*[7]

He's right. The American Declaration of Independence proclaims that people have equal worth and an equal right to life, liberty, and happiness. It says: *"We hold these truths to be self-evident."* The fact is, however, that for those parts of the world which lack a Judeo-Christian heritage, e.g. Africa and Asia, these truths are not at all evident; they are actually quite foreign.[8] The idea that a prince and a pauper should both suffer the same consequence for the same felony is not self-evident for much of humanity. Notions of equality of worth, equality in law, and equality of opportunity are primarily evident in nations founded on Judeo-Christian principles. These biblical principles have undergirded the Western world's legal system, hospital system, education system, and democratic system of governance.

To build society on the platform of secular "common sense" is to build on a continually morphing, unstable platform. The reality is that what is common sense to one generation is not necessarily common sense to the next generation. Each generation defines its own common sense. The moral drift we allow in our generation will be handed down to the next generation, who will view it as normative. They, in turn, will add their own moral drift and hand it on to the next generation. Each ensuing generation will view common sense from the perspective of a position arrived at by moral drift. Common sense is created by culture, so it cannot be asked to be the guardian of culture.

The eighteenth-century Prussian philosopher Immanuel Kant said that reason is the source of morality. He's right. The problem is, without God as a foundation, our reasoning (and therefore our morality) continually changes. The American philosopher and historian Will Durant wrote an eleven-volume work with his wife, Ariel, called *The Story of Civilization*. As a result of his research, he concluded: "*There is no significant example in history, before our time, of a society successfully maintaining moral life without the aid of religion.*" This is a hugely significant statement. The strident atheists, humanists, and secularists of our time are asking us to create a society in which there is no God, when no such society has ever been shown to work well.

Jonathan Sacks voices a similar concern to that of Durant:

> *I have not yet found a secular ethic capable of*
> *sustaining in the long run a society of strong*
> *communities and families on the one hand, altruism,*
> *virtue, self-restraint, honour, obligation and trust on*
> *the other. A century after a civilisation loses its soul, it*
> *loses its freedom also.*

This is a vital point to make.

Yet Christianity should not be adopted simply for the sake of pragmatism – that is, because it results in a "nicer" society. Christianity only deserves to be embraced if it is true. (Evidence of God in truth will be explored in the next chapter.)

India

Vishal Mangalwadi is a Christian philosopher and social activist. He was born and brought up in Allahabad in northern India. His interest in Christianity was aroused when he noted that the only place of worship at the university he attended in Allahabad was a Christian church. He wondered why this should be, given that Allahabad was a particularly sacred city for both the Muslims and the Hindus. The city was the birthplace of many of Hinduism's holy Scriptures (the Vedas and some of Hindu's grand epics), and it hosted the largest religious festival in the world, the Maha Kumbh Mela, typically attended by a hundred million Hindus. And yet the city's university had only a Christian church.

It occurred to Vishal that Christianity, unlike the local religions, puts a priority on truth and seeks to enrich society. It builds universities. This was enough to prompt him to explore the claims of Jesus Christ.

During my first visit to India, I visited the Christian Medical College and Hospital in Vellore, southern India – one of the most internationally renowned hospitals in Asia. It was founded by Dr Ida Scudder, an American missionary who wanted to build a hospital in which Indian women could be treated by female doctors. Many Indian women were dying, particularly in childbirth, because their husbands would not allow them to be attended by a male doctor. I visited some of the wards in the hospital and frequently heard patients say, "These people really care. They don't mind how poor I am. They do the right thing, not the thing that earns them the most money." It was sobering to be reminded what a rare and precious thing a Christ-like culture is in the world.

My ruminations continued when I saw a beggar in the streets outside. The Hindu culture is not kind to beggars. If a Hindu priest sees a beggar in the street, he may offer alms, as this is a spiritually meritorious thing for him to do. He might also say three things to the beggar:

1. "Your pain is an illusion."

2. "Your low status is your own fault, the product of poor behaviour in a past life."

3. "You must live out your status faithfully and not try to change it."

If a Christian sees the same beggar, he/she might also say three things – three very different things:

1. "Your pain is real."

2. "Your situation is caused in large part by humanity's brokenness, for which we are all responsible."

3. "The Holy Spirit of God in me gives me compassion for you and compels me to help you improve your situation."

All religions are not the same.

Hope and truth

There doesn't seem to be a lot of hope without God. Nobody is doing very well without him. Again, while this doesn't prove God, it should probably encourage us to at least investigate God. Friedrich Nietzsche popularized the idea that "God is dead" and attacked all such notions as meekness and charity, claiming that they were drains on our "will to power". However, his philosophy did not offer much hope. He said, *In reality, hope is the worst of all evils, because it prolongs man's torments.*[9]

Oh dear!

Hope is a precious thing, but hope without truth is simply delusion. Truth is important. It is not the case that every religion or religious practice should be considered valid or good. Some things done in the name of religion are just plain wrong... and the fact that we can say this is significant. It means that we are appealing to an authority of rightness that goes beyond many of the religious activities of humanity.

This raises the issue of what should be tolerated and what should not. There is, of course, a big difference between tolerance and believing that all religions are right. An example is Ayaan Hirsi Ali, the Somali-Dutch activist, atheist, writer, and politician, who feels able to say that female genital mutilation is morally wrong even though it is insisted on by a religion. She has no compunction in ignoring political correctness in order to make a moral judgment about a religious practice.

This hints at the possibility of fundamental truth. Christianity claims that God has revealed this truth through a historically well-attested man called Jesus Christ. He was a wonder-worker with flawless wisdom and morality, and his teaching is available to us in Scripture today. This man died on a cross and rose from the dead – in fulfilment of prophecy written hundreds of years earlier in Scripture. These are concrete claims. They are not myth or saga. They are real… and only real things give hope.

If you add to this the testimony of the transformation that happens to individuals, families, cities, and nations when authentic Christianity is embraced, the truth of Christianity is commended even further.

Adrian Wooldridge, a self-confessed atheist, said that his respect for Christianity has grown as a result of his research into the activity of religious organizations. He said, "*This was partly because of the people I came across who were doing such amazing work to help the poor.*" He goes on to ask, "*Where are the atheists doing anything like that?*"[10]

It's a good question.

The American Catholic philosopher Michael Novak believes that secular historians have cut off one of the two wings by which the American eagle flies. The wing that has been clipped is the nation's foundation on God. He says that the generation that founded America "*relied upon this belief*". Faith was an indispensable part of the American story.[11] When American historians assembled 15,000 writings from the period of their nation's foundation, they discovered that they included 3,154 citations from the Bible. This was nearly four times as many as the next most popularly quoted authority.

It would seem that the Bible is the soul of Western civilization. Without it, we are left to the heartless, chilly winds of Nietzsche's "will to power", the motivation that drives human ambition and the quest to reach the highest possible position of power in life. Fyodor Dostoevsky reminds us: "*If there is no God, everything is permissible.*"[12]

Nature is pragmatic

Organisms in the plant and animal world will generally seek to kill off anything that threatens their ability to thrive. This includes eating other organisms in order to live. In this dangerous world, everything comes under the all-consuming instinct to dominate and thrive.

When human societies discard Christianity, they invariably default to the behaviour of the plant and animal world.

Vishal Mangalwadi was imprisoned a number of times in India because he promoted the education and social wellbeing of the poor. Some high caste Indians in authority felt that their exclusive claim on status and power was being threatened by him, so they locked him up. One police chief even promised to kill him if he continued to help a poor community repair roofs that had been shattered by a hailstorm.[13]

When Christian principles are absent, you get the killing fields. When Christian principles are absent because the church has been corrupted or muzzled, Auschwitz happens. When Christian principles are absent, it becomes expedient to kill 30 million people through starvation in order to institute a collective farming ideology in China. Without the morality, hope, and principles of Christianity, humanity falls back into the harsh pragmatism of the animal and plant kingdom.

This Machiavellian pragmatism allows you to do anything that is necessary to stay in power. It allowed a French queen and a Pope (for goodness' sake!) to conspire together to murder tens of thousands of Huguenots on St Bartholomew's Day in 1572. It allowed laws to be passed that resulted in the murder of 6 million Jews. It allowed 30,000 people perceived as a political threat to "go missing" in Argentina between 1976 and 1983.

If society is not guarded by a respect for God, then whoever has power wins. If society is not guarded by godly principles, Hitler's National Socialism is a logical outcome. If society is not guarded by a respect for God, it makes perfect sense for your values to be those of the animal kingdom. There is no right to life in this pragmatic world, only the "law of the jungle". If your life gets in the way of my ambitions, I will kill you or enslave you. This is what happens in human societies without an authentic Christian foundation. The truth is, when people stop ruling "under God", they will seek to be like God.

Christianity understands that God is the ultimate authority. The American Pledge of Allegiance describes America as "*one nation under God*", not "one nation under a president or king". President Nixon discovered that he was not above the law regarding the Watergate affair. The law of the people, under God, stood over him.

The significance of this is: If you reject God, you condemn yourself to be ruled by those who are driven by selfish ambitions and a lust for power. This inevitably causes a lot of people to be oppressed. It is significant that people generally move (as refugees or migrants) away from a nation without the values of a Christian heritage to one that has these values. They seek that nation's safety, civility, justice, and prosperity. My own country of Australia has had to institute tough, and I might say contentious, immigration policies in order to stem the flow of immigrants from Sri Lanka, the Middle East, and Asia.

However, many Western nations with a Christian heritage are now losing that heritage. Their people are turning away from Christianity to atheism, or to one of the non-demanding, pluralistic, self-designed religions.

I'm not sure that this bodes well for a nation's ability to continue to be a refuge for those seeking its justice, order and hope.

Losing our spiritual heritage

Our age is one in which people are shedding traditional values and giving up on the idea that anything is fundamentally true. Today's generation is letting its spiritual heritage slip through its fingers. This is no small thing. Our ancestors fought and died for the values that dragged us from an anarchic, fear-laden, truth-eschewing, culturally desolate, justice-avoiding, meaning-ignorant culture… into a civilization based on the Christian ethic of truth, justice, hope, and meaning.

It would be nice to think that our current civilization might be the first that did not commit cultural suicide by self-destructing from within. Historians tell us that all cultures do this when they turn away from the optimism, values, and certainties that caused them to grow.

The symptoms of the postmodern age that now pervade the West give little confidence that we are doing anything other than self-destructing. Patricia Waugh, Professor of English at Durham University, wrote about this phenomenon, saying:

> *The postmodern age [is]… one dominated by anxiety,*
> *irrationalism and helplessness. In such a world,*
> *consciousness is adrift, unable to anchor itself to any*
> *universal ground of justice, truth or reason.*[14]

The twentieth-century Methodist theologian Eli Stanley Jones summarizes this state, saying:

> *The modern man sighs and says: "There are no*
> *absolutes; they have all been dissolved in the acids of*
> *modern thinking… there are not supposed to be any*
> *absolutes – we are born into the relative, live in the*
> *relative, and die in the relative. It is all a vast question*
> *mark."*[15]

A question mark is a poor substitute for meaning and identity. No wonder our children are reaching for society's analgesics – and society is happy enough to provide them. It feeds our kids on the empty calories of TV, video fantasy, media banality, cultural crassness, Facebook, and Twitter. Our children have become mesmerized by today's cultural gatekeepers: commercialism and the media. As a result, talent has given way to notoriety, the guilty claim to be victims, sentimentality has replaced spirituality, sensationalism has driven out substance, expedience has replaced principle, and commentary is lauded over initiative. There is now massive confusion about what family is, what sexuality is, what gender is, what truth is, and where hope is to be found. Optimism, confidence, and truth have trickled through people's fingers and left them with nothing bigger than themselves to believe in.

The Roman Empire committed cultural suicide by cutting itself adrift morally – particularly with regard to women and children. As a result, it lost certainty and hope, and began to embrace things dark and negative. Some people are suggesting that we are seeing a similar Nihilism emerging today in the West's penchant for body piercing, tattoos, and the emaciated, drugged-up look adopted by some of today's fashion models.

Some may disagree and insist that the future looks wonderful, and "Isn't the younger generation so much better than us?" It is trendy, populist stuff that may gain a ripple of applause for its political correctness, hubris and positivity... but it is a lie. In Australia, suicide is the leading cause of death for people aged between fifteen and forty-four. Its culture is dominated by anxiety and hedonism.

Western atheists have much in common with rebellious teenagers. Having been safely nurtured by the Christian culture of their parents, they now rebel, seeking their own way. Their parents can only look on and be afraid for a generation that is turning its back on ultimate meaning, truth, goodness, and hope.

And speaking of teenagers... let's talk about sex.

Sex, society, and God

Is God good for sex?

For many years, I was a research biologist. My studies in this area indicated that there are two extreme strategies for sex in the animal kingdom – with variations on the theme in between.

One extreme is the philosophy of the rutting wildebeest. This is a winner-takes-all philosophy where the strongest male gets to service the females in the herd. The advantage of this strategy is that the genes for strength are the ones that get passed on to the next generation. It is, however, not an equitable arrangement. There are a lot of very frustrated male wildebeests! It is also relationally sterile: there's not much love. The objective is mechanical coupling rather than the fostering of caring relationships.

Whenever anything like this philosophy is adopted in human civilization, it fosters competition and inequality. The rich and wealthy have many wives, and the poor have none. Where polygamy is practised, there is also competition over who will be the favoured "number one wife", and there is anxiety from the wives over the status of their children. Love (certainly equal love for all wives) is not given a high priority. Polygamy is an arrangement primarily orientated towards the power and status of men.

The other sexual philosophy in the animal kingdom is demonstrated by one of the most comical and raucous of Australian birds, the galah. It mates for life. One of the saddest sights you see on the side of Australian roads is a galah standing beside the carcass of its dead mate who has been killed by a car. And one of the most endearing sights is watching two of them groom each other's necks in a bonding ritual.

The strength of this approach to sex is that it allows a rapid build-up of numbers. It does so because almost every adult is engaged in sexual activity. This is advantageous when numbers need to increase quickly to take advantage of favourable conditions.

Where this approach to sexuality has been adopted by human civilization, it has fostered a quality of love that results in lifelong commitment, greater joy for more individuals, and greater sexual activity in a community.

There is a rightness about this arrangement that resonates with our very being. There may be biological reasons for this feeling, but what can definitely be said is that it is entirely consistent with Christianity, which emphasizes the primacy of relationships. Christianity teaches that God created the universe so that he could include more within the orbit of his love and include us in his community. It was because he wanted to rescue humanity back into relationship with himself that Jesus came to die on a cross. Relationships are therefore the most important thing in the universe. As such, it is not hard to guess which sexual philosophy – that of the wildebeest or the galah – is considered to be good and godly.

Human beings certainly seem happier when they have one partner for life. It is perhaps significant that refugees are generally leaving societies in which the wildebeest philosophy is practised, to embrace the civility of those nations in which the galah philosophy is practised.

Hurrah for the galah!

Kiroth's Bible

The partly burnt, soot-stained page of a Bible is framed and hanging on the wall above my desk. It once belonged to a man named Kiroth. In December 2007, he was part of a group of Christians who ran from their village of Bakingia in the Indian state of Orissa because they and their fellow believers were being attacked, and their houses burnt, by Hindu extremists. Kiroth and his brother decided to turn back in order to retrieve their beloved Bibles. Kiroth managed to recover his badly burnt Bible and rejoin the other displaced Christians hiding in the jungle. Tragically, though, his brother was caught by the Hindus and hacked into pieces.

I look at the page from Kiroth's Bible whenever I am tempted to be careless about my Christian heritage.

Conclusion

The idea that humanism can come up with a robust morality that is able to replace Christian values is a theory that has not yet proved true in history. Such claims should therefore be treated with extreme caution. To trade something that has proved its worth for something that has no history of ever working would seem to be a distinctly odd form of madness.

If religion is discarded, there remains no mechanism to define what is good and just. All that is left is pragmatism. As the sinful bent of humanity will never allow complete equality and justice for everyone, the law of the jungle must inevitably become the default behaviour. The Christian cultural commentator Charles Colson said:

> *If there is no truth – no objective standards of what is good or just and, therefore, no standard of what is unjust – then… tyranny, either from the unrestrained passions of the majority or from the ruthless dictator, invariably follows.*[16]

There is simply no basis for believing the modernist dictum that we are reinventing ourselves to be ever more moral beings who are less dependent on God. Such facile, modernist thinking should have bled to death on our bloody battlefields and in our torture chambers. Only the intellectually lazy and those who are naive can believe such fiction.

In reality, humanists and secularists who want to banish God from society are parasitic on their Christian heritage. They lay claim to its principles (for example, the "golden rule") without understanding that it was a Christian culture that gave rise to it.

Godly principles are a gift from God to us. We follow them imperfectly, but we are nonetheless glad that they are there. Biblical principles have proven to be the most reliable and effective guardian of humanity. They have caused nations to thrive socially, morally, educationally, and scientifically.

Proverbs 14:34 says, "*Righteousness exalts a nation.*" This is a profound comment.

There is much evidence of God to be seen in what works best in society.

6

THE EVIDENCE OF GOD IN TRUTH .

Authentic Christians are passionate about truth. They have to be, because Christians believe that God requires it, embodies it, defines it... and *is* it. Christianity, more than any other religion, is preoccupied with truth. Certainly, Jesus was. He said "*I tell you the truth*" about eighty times in the Gospels, which is a pretty fair indication of the importance that he placed on it.

The primacy of truth is not easily found in other religions. Hinduism is essentially based on mythology, Buddhism on mysticism, and Islam on a private revelation that others can't verify. Islam is a religion that must be forced on others by the threat of the sword. At the very least, the obligation of *dhimmi* requires Islam to dominate other faiths.

The new, syncretistic religions of today, such as New Age, are equally careless about truth. Postmodernism goes even further and has given up on the idea of truth altogether.

In contrast to this, Christianity is vitally concerned with truth. Christianity, you see, is not just a faith, just one among many; it is faith based on truth. In other words, Christianity is evidence-based. If it could be shown that any of the essential truths about Jesus are false, Christianity would be completely invalid. Notwithstanding the cancerous invasions of deism into Christian institutions in the guise of liberal theology, Christianity is founded on the life, death, and resurrection of Jesus in history. Wherever the institutional church has forgotten this, it has emptied its churches, lost its passion for mission, and found itself unable to offer anything in the way of hope. It has simply preached moralism.

Christianity is palpably not just a philosophy.

This is not readily understood by those viewing Christianity from other cultures where they are used to thinking of faith as a philosophy, or as something even more esoteric – a badge that defines their cultural identity. I remember a Chinese student speaking to me with bewilderment and amazement after a lecture I'd given on science and faith. He wanted to insist that Christianity "is just a Western philosophy... and who is to say that it is any better than the philosophy of another culture?" It took a while for him to understand that Christianity is neither Western, nor is it a philosophy. Fundamentally, it is about truth.

At the heart of Christianity are these truth claims: While all major religions have prophets who will help you find God, Christianity is about God finding us. While all major religions tell you what you must do in order to reach God, Christianity is about accepting what God has done to reach you. While most religions have prophets who claim to point to God, Jesus Christ made it clear that he was God. Everything centres on these truth claims.

Dealing with a red herring

Before we go any further, let's deal with a red herring. It is one that usually pops up in a debate about Christian truth. Some raise the very reasonable objection that there are people who call themselves Christians and they are evil. Most of us, sadly, will have come across those who claim to be Christians but have not lived up to it. The fact is that all Christians are a "work in progress" and all of us need God's continual forgiveness. Having said that, I also want to suggest that not everyone who calls themselves a Christian may necessarily be one. Being a Christian actually requires obedience to Christ. It is therefore important to be discerning. After all, a mouse living in a cookie jar does not make it a cookie!

In our discussion of truth, what needs to be addressed is not primarily the good or bad behaviour of alleged Christians, but whether the life, death, and resurrection of Jesus (as witnessed to in the Bible) is true.

What is truth?

It's worth asking, at this point, what truth actually is. Truth is a concept that has been found to be useful. It has enabled us to trade, find a mate, and live in community without being killed. But is truth simply a useful concept that allows communities of *Homo sapiens* to get along? Is truth good only because it is useful – or is it something that is inherently good? Pushing this question even further… Is truth good because it is godly? Do we find evidence of God in the notion of truth?

Let's begin by talking about where truth comes from.

We discover the truth about how things are made and how things work by being curious about our environment. This curiosity leads us to understand our environment better and reap the benefits from doing so. It's worth noting that the drive to do this is not exclusively a human phenomenon. Many animals exhibit curiosity and a desire to know the true status of things in their environment. However, what about moral and spiritual truth, the truth that moves beyond the "how" and "when" to the "who" and "why"? Where does that come from? Is this a truth that we are invited to uncover? Is it something that is divinely encouraged, or is it simply a human construct invented to help us cope with the meaninglessness of our existence?

It is fair to say that some claims about gods and the divine status of things have been entirely human concoctions. Fortunately, our intellect is such that we are usually able to expose such follies and distortions of truth... given enough time and information.

What is indisputable is that there does seem to be a gravitational pull within humanity that causes us to seek a truth, a significance, and a reason for being that is bigger than we are. We suspect there is a sense of rightness in truth that is bigger than social pragmatism. It is significant that only humans can defy their genes and make moral choices about truth... to the point that some are even prepared to die for it.

The relevance of this is that if you are going to stake your life on truth, you had better be very sure you have the right truth! Humanity, sadly, can get this dreadfully wrong – as the existence of suicide bombers attests.

Right belief

It is amazing how often you meet people who say they don't believe in the existence of a historical Jesus, but who are firmly convinced about the existence of intelligent life on other planets. When I think about all the historical evidence for Jesus' existence, some even from non-Christian historians of the time (such as Josephus and Tacitus), I am amazed. It brings to mind the celebrated comment attributed to G.K. Chesterton: "*It used to be believed that if you stopped believing in God, you stopped believing in anything. Alas, the truth is much worse. When you stop believing in God, you start to believe everything.*"[1]

Right belief is important.

Having a right belief about God and having an opinion about God are not the same. To have an opinion about God does not make you an expert. Being an expert requires having the courage to seriously seek out truth. Similarly, to have an opinion about God does not make you right. Being right requires you to explore the facts. Only when you do this can you learn the truth about God and who you are. Australian Aborigines have a belief that a person remains a child (regardless of their age) until they know their story. I invite you to know your story.

Pontius Pilate once famously asked Jesus, "*What is truth?*" (John 18:38). This self-serving, political pragmatist thought truth was impossible to find, and he was bemused that Jesus of Nazareth, who was on trial before him, should claim to embody it.

Many feel like Pilate regarding the issue of whether spiritual truth exists. With there being some 4,800 religions in the world today, this is perhaps understandable. It helps explain why the postmodernists of today have largely given up on the idea of truth, preferring instead whatever works for them in their context. They don't believe there is any ultimate spiritual truth. Fundamentally, we are biological machines dancing to the tune of our genes, which, in turn, are simply a chance conglomeration of atoms.

I was once asked, when recording a radio series in Sydney, why I thought Christianity was true. It's an interesting question to ponder when tens of thousands of people are waiting for your answer. From memory, I said:

> *Christianity has credibility because it is historically true, morally true, sociologically true, experientially true, and scientifically true. If it should fail on any aspect of truth, Christianity is a lie. Whilst other religions can be challenged on some of these areas, there is good, objective evidence that authentic Christianity has retained its integrity in all of them.*

It is significant that Christianity has at its heart a person who said, "*I am... the truth*" (John 14:6). As such, Christianity is not simply a philosophical crutch that people hold on to because they are frightened of the alternative. It is something, or more correctly some*one*, in whom we believe because there is good evidence to suggest that we should.

The extraordinary order of our universe gives us a gentle invitation to look for truth... and the coming of God to us as Jesus makes this invitation a deeply personal one.

My genes made me do it

The idea that humankind is in any way special is being challenged in our time. In his book *The Selfish Gene* the Oxford biologist Richard Dawkins says we are not significant. We are nothing more than slaves to our genes, which craft living bodies around them in order to perpetuate themselves. We are helplessly controlled by our genes, which confer on us the animal instincts that we have. This sort of thinking has given rise to the increasingly common excuse, "Don't blame me; my genes made me do it."

Abdication of moral responsibility in favour of basal animal instincts is very much the vogue at present. The convicted murderer Tony Mobley had a long history of violent behaviour. During his trial in 1994 his attorney argued that he was not responsible for his behaviour because it was possibly due to a serotonin deficiency caused by his genetic make-up. The judge was not persuaded.[2]

Fundamentally, humans have the capacity to embrace what is good and true because they have a real choice – not just because they have the right chemical composition floating about their system. It seems that our genes can result in a tendency, but not a tyranny.

A dangerous proposition

Let's put forward a dangerous proposition: If God is true (and I admit, that is a big "if"), then the only way for anyone to dismiss him is to embrace untruth. The pertinent question is: Do we find atheists embracing untruth to attack the idea of God? If there is a general climate of demonstrable untruth in atheistic attacks on God, then that, in itself, would be a pointer to the probability of God.

Personally, I think that pointer exists.

As a pastor and theologian who is sometimes called to debate with atheists, I have been appalled at the historical fiction some of them believe – even atheists who are very eminent in their field. Quite why they feel it is acceptable to be careless with truth when attacking Christianity puzzles me. To prop up their atheistic convictions they trot out apocryphal tales that are, at best, exaggerations, and at worst, lies.

In no particular order, here are a few:

Church clerics refused to look through Galileo's telescopes to see evidence of scientific truth in the night sky.

No, as we saw in Chapter 2, it was the Aristotelians who refused to look. The clerics quite enjoyed looking through Galileo's telescopes. Some of them even used telescopes for their own research.

The fathers of modern science were not churchmen.

Actually, most of them were, including Copernicus, Galileo, Francis Bacon, Robert Boyle, and Isaac Newton.

Some atheists insist that Newton was more of a Deist than a Christian. (A Deist believes that God is simply an impersonal being who created the universe and then left it to its own devices.)

To say this risks trivializing Newton's deep, abiding, and passionate belief in God. Although he struggled with the conventional Christian understanding of the Trinity, Newton was a serious student of the Bible and published several theological works. Even in his magisterial work *Principia Mathematica* he exhibited his devotion to God. He wrote:

> *This most beautiful system of the sun, planets, and comets, could only proceed from the counsel and dominion of an intelligent and powerful Being… This Being governs all things, not as the soul of the world, but as Lord over all.[3]*

Newton believed that God was everywhere fully present. He wrote, "*God is the same God, always and everywhere. He is omnipresent not virtually only, but also substantially.*"[4] Newton was scathing of any idea that God could not be responsible for the diversity of life that existed. He wrote, "*All that diversity of natural things which we find suited to different times and places could arise from nothing but the ideas and will of a Being.*"[5] It was actually the French mathematician and astronomer Pierre-Simon Laplace who was responsible for developing Newton's theories into a Deist philosophy… which brings us to another atheist claim.

Napoleon once asked Laplace where God fitted into his mathematical work, and Laplace replied, famously, "Sir, I have no need of that hypothesis."

Atheists have seized on this comment to support their ideology. Their folly in doing so is well answered by the Oxford mathematician and philosopher John Lennox, who wrote:

> *Of course God did not appear in Laplace's*
> *mathematical description of how things work, just as*
> *Mr. Ford would not appear in a scientific description*
> *of the laws of internal combustion. But what does that*
> *prove? That Henry Ford did not exist? Clearly not.*
> *Neither does such an argument prove that God does*
> *not exist.[6]*

The humiliation of Samuel Wilberforce, Bishop of Oxford, by Thomas Huxley and Joseph Hooker at a meeting of the British Association at Oxford on 30 June 1860 was a key victory for atheists.

In fact, the protagonists in the debate were not even the main billing for that night. The main speaker was Professor John Draper from New York University, who gave a boring speech in which he expounded on aspects of Darwin's theory. Wilberforce had tried to lighten the proceedings by turning to Huxley and asking whether it was on his grandfather's or his grandmother's side that he was descended from an ape – a statement which Huxley savaged.[7]

Huxley's supporters later inflated this exchange to the point of legend, even though its impact was so minimal at the time that no mention was made of it in any publication for twenty years. It was only then that triumphalist accounts of the debate began to appear, including a very uncomplimentary one about Wilberforce from Mrs Isabella Sidgewick that was published in *Macmillan's Magazine*. Her view belied the fact that Wilberforce had always thought Darwin to be a "capital fellow" (despite his dismay at Darwin's evolutionary ideas) and that he had written an extensive review of *On the Origin of Species*, which Darwin thought was significant enough to cause him to modify his discussion at several points.[8]

Charles Darwin was an atheist.

The man atheists like to champion as one of their own, perhaps more than anyone else, is Charles Darwin. So, let me quote again from a letter he wrote in 1879: "*I have never been an atheist in the sense of denying the existence of God.*"[9] Rather embarrassingly, Richard Dawkins didn't know this until Cardinal George Pell apprised him of the fact on prime time Australian television on 9 April 2012.

If God exists, truth should point people to him… and lies should point people away from him. It is therefore good to avoid distortions of truth and be well informed. This brings to mind a rueful comment from C.S. Lewis when he reflected on the devastating impact informed Christian literature had on his atheism. He wrote: "*In reading Chesterton, as in reading MacDonald, I did not know what I was letting myself in for. A young man who wishes to remain a sound Atheist cannot be too careful of his reading.*"[10]

How truthful is someone who is arguably the world's leading atheist?

It's worth looking at the "truth" claims of the Oxford biologist Richard Dawkins, as he has been one of the frontrunners for atheism in recent decades. (Others have included the British-

American Marxist Christopher Hitchens; the polemicist and journalist Sam Harris; and the American philosopher and neuroscientist Daniel Dennett.)

Richard Dawkins is particularly well known for his book *The God Delusion*. It is an ungracious and unscholarly diatribe against faith that does not deserve to be taken seriously, despite the fact that it begins with pages of people who have endorsed it. For reasons that will soon become apparent, these people should each hang their head in shame.

Dawkins makes two central claims. The first is that atheists are better moral guardians of planet Earth than people with faith. His second is that faith in God is not scientifically reasonable.

Are these claims true?

Is religion bad for planet Earth?

Dawkins begins his book by asking us, in the words of John Lennon, to "imagine" a utopian world in which there is no religion.[11] Implicit in this invitation is the claim that religion has been the cause of most wars in history.

A cursory look at history shows this to be untrue. In the last century, 180 million people died as a result of conflict. Some 65 million of them were killed in two world wars, and a staggering 74 million were killed by the very unchristian Communism of Lenin, Stalin, and Mao.[12] The reality is that the most humane, just and successful nations in history have been those which faithfully reflect the Judeo-Christian ethic.

False representation

Dawkins is intellectually dishonest when he compiles a catalogue of fundamentalists and fanatics, and tries to pass these off as typical Christians. Driven by his ideological convictions, he represents Christians in an extreme, caricatured form that in no way reflects normality. In his determination to believe that religion is bad for the world, Dawkins lumps the morally repugnant, truth-denying practices of some religions with Christianity. By so doing, he makes a totally inadequate distinction between a hate-crazed suicide bomber and Mother Teresa. This brings to mind a comment by the American psychologist David Myers, who said: "*To judge religious faith by vulgar caricatures that would make a first-year theology student wince is like judging science by eugenics, nuclear warheads and chemical pollutants.*"[13]

While repudiating the toxic caricature of Christians by Dawkins, it must be acknowledged that Christian institutions have always been deeply flawed organizations that have often lived in contradiction to the teachings of Jesus Christ. It is perhaps significant that Jesus' most vehement opponents were religious leaders. However, Dawkins seems unable to concede the obvious truth that if Christians act in a way that is contrary to their founder's teachings, then the problem is their unfaithfulness, not his teaching. Only if they are acting in a way taught by Christ can Christianity be blamed. To blame Christianity for unchristian behaviour makes as much sense as blaming science for fraudulent scientists.

Do scientists have faith?

Dawkins tries to say that very few credible scientists are Christians. His source of authority is the personal opinion of fellow atheists such as James Watson (of DNA fame). This is ridiculous. He has ignored authentic research such as that done by Larson and Witham, who discovered that 40 per cent of scientists in America believe in a God to whom they can pray with the expectation of receiving an answer.[14]

Dawkins chooses not to give much credit to the many eminent

academics (including scientists) in his own university who are convinced that God exists, including Alister McGrath (chemistry and theology), John Lennox (mathematics), and Keith Ward (philosophy and theology). Nor has he seen fit to report on the extraordinary increase in the number of shared chairs of theology and science in the world's academic institutions in the last thirty years.[15]

In his zeal to discredit Christianity, Dawkins is often just plain wrong. He repeatedly says, "*Jesus (if he existed)...*", without acknowledging that no serious scholars question the existence of Jesus. Two almost contemporary (and, I might say, non-Christian) historians, Josephus and Tacitus, wrote about Jesus.

Dawkins also claims that the commandment to love your neighbour "*really meant to just love other Jews*". However, Jesus' parable about the Good Samaritan in Luke 10:25–37 teaches exactly the opposite.

Unbelievably, Dawkins quotes a speech by Hitler in which the despot claims to be a Christian.[16] Given the hundreds of thousands of Christians Hitler exterminated on account of their faith, this is obscene. The true conviction of the Nazi party regarding Christianity, detailed in reports by General William Donovan from the Nuremberg war trials, showed that they planned to eliminate authentic (biblical) Christians.[17]

Dawkins' bigotry and lack of objective balance is deeply disturbing. He speaks of Christianity's "*loathing of women*".[18] He does this despite the following facts:

- Jesus honoured women.
- The Apostle Paul honoured over twelve influential women in the church and taught that men and women were equal before God.[19]

- Christians played a key role in winning the vote for women in the West.[20] The Women's Christian Temperance Union, for example, were influential in winning women the vote in the late nineteenth century in America, New Zealand, and Australia.

Dawkins can't resist attacking Christianity by claiming that it fostered and encouraged slavery. This claim is so absurd, unbalanced, and unjust that it has provoked a stinging attack from Melvyn Bragg, a well-known English broadcaster and author who claims no religious faith at all. Bragg points out that it was Christians such as William Wilberforce and John Newton who spearheaded the emancipation of slaves, not atheists. Not only that but Christianity played a key role in helping slaves understand their right to freedom and gave them hope that someday that right might be realized.[21]

Let me pause here and say that Dawkins's claims are serious untruths. We are not talking about differences of opinion here; we are talking about genuine untruth.

Alarmingly, some of Dawkins's convictions are based on no evidence at all. For example, he tries to dismiss the mystery of the universe by claiming that evolutionary processes applicable to non-biological objects such as molecules and galaxies will eventually be found. In a most unscientific way, he asks us to believe this even though no such mechanisms have been discovered.

By any stretch of the imagination, this is not science. It is ideology run amok. Dawkins asks us to accept the miracle of existence simply by shrugging our shoulders and saying it was an improbable event that must have happened because we are here.[22]

Failing at theology

Dawkins is on sound ground when he does authentic biology. However, he makes a terrible theologian. He ridicules the God of the Old Testament and thinks that by so doing, he is discrediting Christianity. This makes as much sense as a theologian ridiculing science because of the teaching of medieval scientists. Dawkins fails to understand that scriptural truth, like scientific truth, is progressive. It builds up with time as God reveals more truth. Scriptural truths only reach their fullness in Christ Jesus.[23] Christ is therefore the lens through which we must interpret all of Scripture. Perhaps because Dawkins is unable to cope with Jesus' radical life of love, he barely mentions him other than to make a few disparaging remarks.

Not surprisingly, Dawkins finds the concept of the Trinity impossible to grasp. He doesn't seem to realize that while God has chosen to reveal quite a lot about himself, God has to be more than our minds *can* conceive – if he is to be more than our minds *have* conceived. Logically, there has to be some mystery to God.

Teapots and other silly things

Sadly, Dawkins is just one of a long line of atheists saying silly things about Christianity.

The atheist Bertrand Russell scorned the idea of Christianity, saying that there was no proof it was true. He used a spectacularly unfair analogy to ridicule the idea of God's existence: Since we can't prove that there isn't a tiny teapot circling the Sun like a planet (a teapot too small to see), we have to allow that such a teapot could be circling the Sun. Russell says that this is the sort of reasoning Christians display as they insist we have to allow for the possibility of God because he can't be disproved.[24]

This sort of argument is crass and intellectually dishonest.

To state the banally obvious, a teapot is a man-made object built for brewing and pouring tea. By its definition, by its origin and by its function, it is not a planet.

A universe that compels many people to take the existence of God seriously is quite a different matter. It is riddled with codes, order, and mind-bogglingly unlikely occurrences that have resulted in the existence of intelligent life. If we look to find a reasonable cause for all this, we can only use the pattern that we have already found to work – the law of cause and effect. This suggests that the universe is shot through with signs of a mind. Nothing else explains it. What we observe is entirely consistent with there being a rational mind behind it all. So much so that any other theory – such as one that allows for everything coming from nothing as a result of nothing – can be considered unlikely, if not impossible.

The universe is not a blank page with nothing on it to give us a clue as to its origin. The evidence of what does exist means we are not free to believe any crass thing – as Bertrand Russell would have us believe. The fact that the universe appears designed to allow for an outcome suggests that there is a divine mind behind it.

Christianity is reasonable; tiny teapots flying round the Sun are not. If atheism requires the intellectual absurdity and dishonesty shown by Bertrand Russell's analogy, it deserves to be ignored.

Atheists require that certain features of the universe (the fact that it exists and the nature of its existence) be accorded no significance in order to allow them to believe that God doesn't exist. This, I submit, is worse than holding to a belief on the basis that there is no possible way to disprove it. Atheists are holding to a belief despite there being indicators to the contrary.

The very nature of the universe should at least prompt some humility from atheists. If I were asking you to believe that there is a tiny teapot flying around the Sun as a miniature planet, you would be justified in asking, "Where's the evidence?" But if I say there is good, scientific, logical evidence of a mind behind the universe, that is another thing all together. If I back that up further with the historical record of Jesus – and if I add in the claims Jesus made about himself, the morality of Jesus, and the transformative power of authentic Christianity – then I can know quite a lot. To forbid me to claim this knowledge as truth is ideological bullying. It is censorship of a reasonable position. You may choose not to understand it; you may choose not to investigate it; you may choose not to embrace it... but if you forbid it, you are a tyrant.

Abusing Scripture

There is no integrity in atheists reading Scripture selectively, putting the worst possible spin on it so that meanings are imposed on the text that it was never written to teach. I have seen this done by atheists wanting to denigrate the teachings of Scripture. This sort of behaviour has more in common with lascivious schoolboys reading a piece of literature, imposing emphases and double entendres on it so that they turn it into pornography.

There can only be two reasons why atheists do this: perversity or ignorance. There is little that can be done with wilful perversity, but we are able to address ignorance. Can I respectfully remind atheists who have formal scientific training that a PhD in physics or biology does not qualify you to speak authoritatively on theology. You would be justly miffed if theologians dared to speak on science with the same abandon. While the essence of God's truth can be understood by a small child, infinitely greater skill and training is required to understand the full theological significance of scriptural teaching, particularly on difficult subjects.

Having said this, let me acknowledge two things. The first is that there are a few theologians of the biblical literalist persuasion who do try to meddle with objective scientific truth. All I can say about this is: I'm sorry. They are wrong.

The second is the sad reality that too many theologians have not served Christianity very well.

Having said that, it remains reasonable to ask people not to distort Scripture for their own purposes... and not to speak about things of which they are ignorant.

If anyone claims that truth is important, they need to be truthful.

Is faith scientifically credible?

A key claim by Dawkins is that belief in God is not scientifically credible. He is quite wrong. Many Christians celebrate science but believe that faith puts science in a wider context of meaning. Science alone fails to explain why the universe exists, why it is so ordered, and why we have the necessary skills to understand it.

Christians understand that science and theology answer different questions. This means that the two disciplines do not compete. However, they also acknowledge that all truth, including scientific truth, has its origin in God. As such, theology and science cannot be in opposition, but must be mutually supportive.

Evolution is a remarkably good and well-attested theory that explains much of what we see. Evolutionary science is therefore okay. However, the philosophical ideology that Dawkins brings to evolution, coloured by his atheism and lack of academic integrity, is not. It is somewhat galling when atheists fracture truth historically, philosophically, and theologically, and then claim to be children of the Enlightenment who stand exalted on the pillar of empirical truth, high above the "fictions" of superstition and religion.

I am the first to acknowledge that there are people of integrity who have intellectual difficulties with Christianity. That said, the sheer volume of carelessness with truth that is shown by many leading atheists brings to mind Jesus' comment, "*Everyone on the side of truth listens to me*" (John 18:37). I can't help but notice that an awful lot of people who don't love truth are not listening to Jesus.

We have said that if God exists, those who want to dismiss him will have to embrace untruth in order to do so. Could it be that the poor behaviour of many of the world's leading atheists points to the possibility of God?

The bleakness of being nothing more than a machine

Dan Dennett, Richard Dawkins, Sam Harris, and Christopher Hitchens suggest that science is totally concerned with the material – that we operate and exist only because of the material, and that anything supernatural should be derided and scorned as you would the idea that there are fairies at the bottom of your garden. Anything that exists does so because it is a machine that has built itself up from primordial particles through evolutionary processes – most of which have yet to be discovered.

Their claim that everything can be reduced to a machine makes for a very bleak world.

Darwin didn't much like the idea that his theory of evolution helped promote a reductionist model of human existence. He spoke of being deeply disturbed at the idea that all that was noble and good about humanity was, in reality, just something that derived from primitive animals. Humankind's best endeavours therefore had no significance at all. He wrote to William Graham on 3 July 1881, saying:

> With me, the horrid doubt always arises whether the
> convictions of man's mind, which has been developed
> from the mind of the lower animals, are of any
> value or at all trustworthy. Would anyone trust in
> the convictions of a monkey's mind, if there are any
> convictions in such a mind?[25]

There is nothing very ennobling about reducing the best of human endeavours to tiny subatomic billiard balls bumping into each other. Something in us instinctively knows this to be wrong. Certainly, there is not much joy in considering the paintings of John Constable as mere daubs of pigment that are coloured differently because of their selective adsorption of various wavelengths of light.

The English Romantic poet John Keats wrote a poem called *Lamia* in 1819 in which he complains that science has removed all mystery and meaning from the world. Because Isaac Newton has provided a scientific explanation of the colour spectrum, the rainbow has been "unweaved". Keats writes:

> Do not all charms fly
> At the mere touch of cold philosophy?
> There was an awful rainbow once in heaven:
> We know her woof, her texture; she is given
> In the dull catalogue of common things.
> Philosophy will clip an Angel's wings,
> Conquer all mysteries by rule and line,

Empty the haunted air, and gnomed mine –
Unweave a rainbow, as it erewhile made
The tender-person'd Lamia melt into a shade.

Quantum physics to the rescue!

Happily, we need not despair. The old Newtonian idea of physics, which biologists such as Richard Dawkins largely inhabit, has been superseded by the findings of physicists exploring the quantum world.

As we discussed in Chapter 4, science has moved on from a purely mechanistic view of a material world into something very different. Electrons are no longer considered to be particles that fly around the nucleus of an atom; rather, they inhabit a "probability wave". They exist in a superposition of many states and only collapse into one particular reality when they are observed.

The big question is, of course: When does this happen? When does a quantum system stop existing as a superposition of many possible states and become one thing or the other? Erwin Schrödinger encapsulated the conundrum in a thought experiment known popularly as Schrödinger's cat. (Do an Internet search if you're interested.)

Whatever the answer, what is not in doubt is that quantum physics has killed off any notion that the universe is simply made up of tiny bricks of matter. It now seems that consciousness may be the ultimate reality.

This has relevance for you and me. Regardless of quantum weirdness, at some point or other we have to be us. So, who is observing us to make us collapse into our current reality? Are there multiverses with different options… or could it be that God is observing us?

Quantum physics, it would seem, is entirely consistent with the Christian notion of God. The Oxford philosopher and theologian Keith Ward makes the point that the start of John's Gospel describes Jesus as the *Logos*, which roughly translated means "*the reason and consciousness of God – the one who calls all things into being*".[26]

Explaining away explanations

In a review of Richard Dawkins's *The God Delusion*, Notre Dame philosopher Alvin Plantinga argues that naturalism is self-defeating and cannot be believed rationally. If, as naturalists claim, there is no God guiding the evolutionary process, then there is no reason to think that our cognitive faculties are reliable in giving us true beliefs about the world. As such, any conclusion we reach about what is true, including the claim that evolution is unguided, is untrustworthy. Naturalism, whether it concerns evolution or anything else, is self-defeating and must be given up.[27]

C.S. Lewis makes a similar point:

> *The kind of explanation which explains things away*
> *may give us something, though at a heavy cost. But you*
> *cannot go on "explaining away" for ever: you will find*
> *that you have explained explanation itself away. You*
> *cannot go on "seeing through" things for ever... To "see*
> *through" all things is the same as not to see.*[28]

Two difficulties for atheists

Atheists have two objections to the Christian claim that humankind and planet Earth are significant. It's worth having a look at them because they illustrate the importance of being theologically literate.

Both objections arise because atheists have reduced God to what they would imagine him to be if he were simply a human construct. The truth, however, is that if God exists, he cannot be contained by the ability of the human mind to imagine him.

The first of the two objections is that the universe is 13.79 billion years old. The fact that it is so old must surely mean it is stupid to think that humankind, which has existed for a mere blink of an eye (some 100,000 years), has any special significance at all.

A theologian would answer this by pointing out that while time is significant for us (in that we are creatures locked within time), it is completely irrelevant to God who stands outside of time. So, while the things that happen in time matter to God, time itself is invisible to him.

The second problem atheists have is similar. It is that the universe is unimaginably big. The observable universe is currently thought to be about 92 billion light-years in diameter – and expanding. In fact, it may be infinitely large. As such, it is ridiculous to think that any biological activity on one planet circling a middle-aged star has any significance. The very size of the universe suggests that the Christian claim that humankind is special to a god is preposterous.

Again, it needs to be pointed out that Christians understand that God is omnipresent; he is everywhere fully present. So, while size is a significant and limiting factor for us, it is irrelevant to God.

It should be gently pointed out that if atheists are going to attack the idea of God, they will need to attack the right God, not some time-bound, space-bound human construct. The need to do this is, as Sherlock Holmes would say, "elementary".

A very sensible question to ask is why God has chosen to surround humankind on planet Earth with a universe that is so old in time and large in size.

The biblical answer is that God is showing off. By making things as grand as they are, God is hanging his business card in the heavens for us to read. He has written it in a language that is compelling to stone-age man and to today's astrophysicists.

This is entirely consistent with the three passages in Scripture that invite us to take God seriously as a result of what we see in creation. Psalm 19:1–2 speaks of the splendour of the universe showing the majesty of God; Acts 17:27 teaches that humankind's place in an ordered creation is an invitation to reach out to God; and Romans 1:20 points out that the qualities of creation should prompt us to explore the possibility that it has a divine origin.

Let me tell you about my dog

The human concept of truth is very different to that found in the animal kingdom. It's important to say this, given that some militant atheists are suggesting that we are socially sophisticated animals that have evolved a sense of truth to suit our particular context.

The concept that truth has moral value is uniquely human.

Issues of truth and lies do not, of course, only involve humans. As a biologist, I can tell you that animals are capable of untruth (as it is defined from a human perspective). Insects mimic others in order to predate or escape predation. Dogs under threat will roll over and show their sexual organs to distract an aggressor. They will do this even though sexual desire is the last thing on their mind. Some males of the Australian giant cuttlefish mimic females so that they can get close enough to mate with a female who is being guarded by another male. Animals can display falsehood. Whenever my dog, JJ, is uncertain about how she should respond to me, she will yawn and stretch down on her front paws. It's lies, all lies. Her action is designed to show unconcerned companionship, when in reality she has some concern as to the status of our relationship.

Similarly, JJ can express guilt and fear when she knows that she has done something wrong. She adopts a carping, winsome demeanour designed to help her avoid the consequences, or at least to minimize them.

These are instinctive behaviours designed to help her survive. But metaphysical truth – that which we celebrate and are prepared to die for – is something else entirely.

Why does truth exist? Is our concept of truth simply an evolutionary by-product that is not really worthy of the epithet "good"?

It can get pretty lonely in university campuses in the West for those who think truth is anything other than relative (a handy conviction you adopt on a Monday but which you can change on a Tuesday depending on what you feel works for you at the time).

The postmodern wild-child

It is worth asking: Can anything be true at all? Today's apologists need to understand that any dialogue between science and faith will take place within a postmodern social culture. Some aspects of this are positive. Today's postmodern culture puts a high priority on relationships, cultural relevance, and congruency, but it also has a darker side. Postmodernism scorns the idea that absolute truth exists. All truth is relative. People construct truth to make sense of their experiences. Experience is everything. If a truth is not compatible with an experience someone wants to have, they simply change the truth.

This sort of thinking brings to mind the wrathful comment of the Old Testament prophet Isaiah, who railed against those calling *"evil good and good evil, who put darkness for light and light for darkness..."* (Isaiah 5:20–22).

Postmodern thinking is intensely suspicious of "metanarratives" like the Bible. It considers them to be tools that have been developed to control people. As such, metanarratives should be interrogated to uncover the repressive views that have given rise to them, particularly those which prejudice minority groups.

In truth, very few people consciously adopt hard-edged postmodern thinking. They just allow its influence to waft over them and encourage them into an increasingly secular, morally vacuous lifestyle. Postmodern thinking is a symptom of the angst of a secularizing world that did not get the utopia it had hoped for from modernism. It is a disturbing phenomenon because, in the view of historians such as Arnold Toynbee, it is indicative of a civilization that is in terminal decline. Evidently, these symptoms are found in civilizations committing cultural suicide – which have lost faith in the old certainties that held society together.[29]

Wouldn't it be nice if we could avoid it?

Tolerance: the postmodern mantra

One of the key pillars of postmodern thinking is tolerance. All religions and philosophies must be tolerated, except the morally repugnant ones... which raises the interesting question of who decides what is, and what is not, morally repugnant.

The philosophy of tolerance was articulated by the English poet and polemical author John Milton, at the height of the English Civil War in 1644. He wrote a tract entitled *Areopagitica*, an impassioned philosophical argument in support of free speech. It was prompted by civil antagonism towards him when he was arguing the case for divorce. He did this, rather sadly, following the experience of his own young wife deserting him. In his tract, Milton argues that truth and untruth should be allowed to slug it out in public debate. This would allow truth to be discovered and defined.

Tolerance has changed since then. For Milton, tolerance was a tool that helped uncover truth. Today, tolerance is advocated because of the conviction that there is no absolute truth. Spiritual truth and matters of ultimate meaning are not now taught at our universities. They simply impart information, equipping people to earn a salary but not equipping them for life… or, indeed, for death.

Where comparative religions and philosophies are studied, this is conducted largely as an intellectual exercise – one that looks at different religions almost as if they were sideshow oddities. Institutional political correctness now requires them to consider all religions as being equally valid – a position that condemns all religions, including Christianity, to being delusional follies. For if everything is true, then nothing is true. To put it in philosophical terms: if A can also be non-A, there can be no such thing as truth. Religion is, therefore, nonsense.

There is, therefore, an embargo on seeking truth about the big questions of life in most Western universities. Most are not training people to think about such vital issues as who they are, what is true, or what is good. This is tragic. The British theologian and minister Lesslie Newbigin rues this fact. He believes that relativism, which is not willing to speak about truth but only about "what is true for me", is an evasion of the serious business of living. It is the mark of a loss of nerve in our contemporary culture.[30]

Elephants, humility, and truth

Despite the postmodern climate in which we live, an ache for significance and meaning remains in most of us. But what can we believe? After all, there is a plethora of people claiming this or that to be true. The cries of those peddling crystals, magic, Eastern mysticism, cults, and bizarre alternative spiritual practices seem to mock our search for truth.

Not surprisingly, this has led some to give up searching for spiritual truth. Instead, they seek to dilute the significance of our existence by saying that there must be an infinite number of worlds and intelligences "out there". Our universe just happened by chance to possess the necessary factors that allowed life to develop.

It needs to be said, however, that this argument doesn't actually explain *why* we exist. As we said in Chapter 1, you can't explain a universe by pointing to a multitude of universes any more than you can explain a book by pointing to a library of books. That is simply to avoid the question.

It is also worth noting, in passing, that despite different theories about an infinite number of universes, many scientists believe that this life is all there is – and all scientists agree that there is, as yet, no evidence of intelligent life elsewhere in the universe. The question of why anything exists at all, and why we exist as we do on this planet, remains.

Others simply shrug their shoulders and say that all religions show aspects of truth. The claim that one religion has a monopoly on truth is, in their view, arrogant. Lesslie Newbigin challenges this thinking, saying:

> *There is an admirable air of humility about the*
> *statement that the truth is much greater than any one*

person or religious tradition can grasp. The statement is no doubt true, but it can be used against the truth when it is used to neutralize any affirmation of truth.[31]

When such a statement "*is used to invalidate all claims to discern the truth, it is in fact an arrogant claim*".[32]

He goes on to borrow the analogy we encountered in Chapter 4 – that of a king who watches five blind men examining an elephant. Each man grabs a different part of the elephant and imagines that the whole is similar to whatever object he thinks he is holding. This analogy is often used to point to the need for any one faith to have humility regarding exclusive truth claims. Newbigin points out that to come to this conclusion is to miss the point. It ignores the fact that the king can see the whole elephant – and the five blind men. The king understands the full story perfectly... and has no need to be modest about his claim to understand.

The fact is that Christianity is different from other religions.

On the face of it, it would be outrageous and arrogant to believe that Jesus is the only way to God... except for one rather obvious proviso: unless it were true.

So, is it true?

The statements that Jesus made about himself certainly make it clear that he was not claiming to be merely a prophet.

- He claimed to be able to forgive sins (Mark 2:5).
- He claimed that he would one day judge the world (Matthew 25:31–32).
- He claimed that he would one day raise people up to everlasting life with God (John 5:28–39; 6:39–40, 44, 54; 10:28; 11:25).

- He claimed authority to confer a heavenly kingdom on people (Luke 22:29–30).

- He claimed that to have seen him was to have seen God (John 14:8–9).

- He claimed that whoever receives him receives God (Matthew 10:40).

- He claimed to be worthy of our absolute devotion (Matthew 10:37–39).

- He claimed to have always existed (John 8:58).

- He claimed to be the Christ (Greek), or Messiah (Aramaic), meaning "anointed one" (Mark 14:61–62; John 4:24–26).

Certainly, Jesus' enemies recognized that he was claiming to be God (John 5:18; 10:31–33).

Jesus disturbs us with claims that have to be either rejected or accepted. What he cannot be is one option among many. He has to be reviled or worshipped.

Six days of creation: Adam and Eve… and all that

Christians have been particularly scorned for believing things that are patently untrue regarding the first three chapters of Genesis, which speak about God creating the world.

I have to say, we've deserved it. Too many Christians in this debate have been ungracious to other Christians who hold a different view about how literally the Genesis creation accounts should be understood. Some have also been ungracious to atheists who question how anyone can take these accounts seriously at all.

I am very sorry about this.

It is my hope that what I say next may be of some help if you have been perplexed about the issue.

The first three chapters of Genesis are not primarily concerned with science's "how" and "when", as we have already said, but theology's "who" and "why". The great fathers of the Christian faith understood this to be so. In AD 415, St Augustine wrote a commentary on Genesis in which he said that some sections of the book should be understood metaphorically.[33] His approach was to adopt a literal understanding of a scriptural passage unless it could be established that a metaphorical reading was necessary.

The great Swiss reformer John Calvin (a stickler for God's word if ever there was one!) said that the language used by God in talking about six days of creation was language that he had *accommodated* so that it could be understood by humanity.[34] Therefore, not all of Genesis is literal. As we saw in Chapter 2, Calvin said that the Bible was not a scientific textbook, and wrote, "*He who would learn astronomy and other recondite arts, let him go elsewhere.*"[35]

All good advice.

So, what incontrovertible truths do the first three chapters of Genesis teach that all Christians can rejoice in and say "Amen" to together?

These chapters declare in peerless prose that:

- In an age of many gods, there is only one God.
- In an age when people are worshipping objects in nature, all of nature is created by God.
- In an age when the gods are believed not to care, God thinks his creation is fantastic.
- In an age that fails to explain the reality of evil, evil is rebellion against God.

- In an age that cannot make sense of suffering, suffering is the result of humankind's choice to go down a path that God never intended.

- In an age which despairs of finding justice and which tolerates evil, God declares that he has zero tolerance for evil and will ensure that justice ultimately prevails.

This profound teaching at the start of the Bible is the foundation of all that follows. It is the foundation of the love story in which God reveals himself to humankind and rescues us back to himself through Jesus. This is the place where all Christians can unite with joy and say, "That is true."

According to a South Australian survey in 2001, 80 per cent of tertiary-trained people who do not attend church believe that Christianity is not scientifically credible.[36] In other words, they believe that you have to commit intellectual suicide to be a Christian.

This is deeply concerning.

Christians have no right to obstruct others from coming to faith by requiring them to believe impossible things before they can become a Christian. Some Christian organizations have publicized exaggerated claims aimed at discrediting the evolutionary theory. Many of these claims have not represented the full facts, and a few are plain untrue. This aggressive defence of a literal understanding of Genesis has helped grow a self-authenticating subculture among Christians that is trumpeting the death of evolution as a credible theory. It is not a view that is shared by most scientists.

Some atheistic scientists have been equally careless with truth. They have pointed to the mounting evidence for evolution and thought that by doing so they were discrediting the existence of God. It needs to be pointed out that, while evolution is a plausible mechanism that explains the development of biological diversity, it cannot explain why such a mechanism exists, how the universe began, why it is so amazingly ordered, or why we can understand it.

Some scientists have questioned the ability of the evolutionary theory to explain all the biological complexity that we see in life – and have done so for legitimate scientific reasons. These views should be respected, even though they are not shared by a majority of scientists. No scientific theory should be dismissed on ideological grounds, whether religious or atheistic. All theories need to be held up to rigorous scientific scrutiny so that they can be explored and tested.

Other people have sought to discredit evolutionary theory because they believe that by doing so, they are protecting the status of the Bible as the infallible word of God. This is regrettable, as the opening chapters of Genesis are not primarily concerned with science. As such, those attacking evolutionary theory can end up being guilty of imposing on Scripture a dogma that the original authors (and God) never intended.

The fact is: *All* truth, whether scientific or theological, has its origin in God. Therefore, we must not set scientific truth against theological truth. Both are valid. Science helps us understand "how", and theology helps us understand the broader context science operates in by addressing the issue of "why".

The militant anti-scientific creationism that has resurfaced in the last hundred years is really a cuckoo living in the church's nest. It shouldn't be there. Let me say quickly that many "young Earth" creationists are wonderful, sincere people with integrity. Sadly, however, there is much that lacks integrity coming from people promoting the young Earth position. To name just a few examples:

- Some claim that dinosaur footprints were found next to human footprints in petrified mud.
  No, that's been shown to be a mistake.

- Some claim to have found Noah's ark.
  This claim has actually been made about forty times! All such claims have been shown to be mistakes or frauds. One "discovery" claimed to have found the ark, together with metal nails and the remains of animal pens. It was shown to be completely false on prime time TV. Ouch!

- Some claim huge gaps in the fossil record.
  That's a gross oversimplification.

- Some claim that the speed of light has changed.
  It has since been shown that there is no evidence for this.

- Some claim to have found the wagon wheels of Egyptian chariots that were overwhelmed with water while chasing the Hebrew people across the Red Sea. One of the wheels was said to have been given to an esteemed Egyptian archaeologist for verification.
  No evidence of this has yet come to light.

And so it goes on and on.

These errors appear on church websites, in church magazines, and on Christian bookstalls. Some pastors even allow this misinformation to be preached from their pulpits. What makes these abuses of scientific truth worse is that they are being perpetrated in the name of preserving biblical integrity. If we Christians have any ambition to reach out to educated people with the gospel, we must not block their path to faith by requiring them to believe things that are demonstrably untrue. God is a God of truth, and Christians should reflect it.

Even so, finding truth among the mess of it all can be difficult. I have real sympathy for pastors and ministers who don't have much scientific knowledge. However, there is now information available that can help.[37]

Being truthful about evidence of God

Too often, people give academic reasons for not taking God seriously when, in reality, they are wanting the freedom to pursue their self-interests. This results in them not investigating God very closely. They simply conform lazily to the atheistic culture around them, and form an opinion about God from what they have gleaned from a few TV programmes.

I don't know about you, but if I were God and had built a universe of unimaginable vastness and splendour to get your attention, I'd be pretty grumpy about being dismissed in such a cavalier way.

The motive for not seeking the truth about God varies. For some, it is simply laziness. For others, they dare not entertain the possibility of God for more selfish reasons. Now, don't get me wrong. I have every respect and empathy for those who have legitimate intellectual difficulties with the idea of God – but if you are open to the possibility of finding God, you will at least research the possibility with an open mind. Given the extraordinarily complex nature of the universe around us, surely we owe it to ourselves to investigate its cause with at least some degree of diligence.

… All of which brings us to a beautiful promise: God says in Scripture that "*You will… find me [God] when you seek me with all your heart*" (Jeremiah 29:13).

The question is: Where do we go looking in order to find God?

A very obvious place to begin is creation – the universe around us.

The Bible makes it plain that God expects us to look at creation and draw some conclusions from it regarding his existence. Here are some of the Bible verses that teach this:

> *The heavens declare the glory of God;*
> *the skies proclaim the work of his hands.*
> *Day after day they pour forth speech;*
> *night after night they reveal knowledge.*
> *They have no speech, they use no words;*
> *no sound is heard from them.*
> *Yet their voice goes out into all the earth,*
> *their words to the ends of the world.*
> *In the heavens God has pitched a tent for the sun.*
>
> (Psalm 19:1–4)

> *Yet he has not left himself without testimony: He has*
> *shown kindness by giving you rain from heaven and*
> *crops in their seasons; he provides you with plenty of*
> *food and fills your hearts with joy.*
>
> (Acts 14:17)

> *From one man he made all the nations, that they*
> *should inhabit the whole earth; and he marked out*
> *their appointed times in history and the boundaries of*
> *their lands. God did this so that they would seek him*
> *and perhaps reach out for him and find him…*
>
> (Acts 17:26–27)

> *For since the creation of the world God's invisible*
> *qualities – his eternal power and divine nature – have*
> *been clearly seen, being understood from what has*
> *been made, so that people are without excuse. For*
> *although they knew God, they neither glorified him as*
> *God nor gave thanks to him, but their thinking became*
> *futile and their foolish hearts were darkened. Although*
> *they claimed to be wise, they became fools…*
>
> (Romans 1:20–22)

These verses are essentially saying the same thing: How seriously have you investigated God based on the evidence of what's around you?

Paul's comment in Romans 1:20–22 that people are without excuse if they don't acknowledge God in the evidence of creation has been dismissed as "poor reasoning" – the sort of "primitive" thinking that existed in Paul's time. We don't make judgmental statements like that any more, now that we are "enlightened".

Some care should be taken before we dismiss Paul's thinking and consign it to the waste bin of historical anachronisms. It is indeed true that Paul speaks from the perspective of the worldview of the time – but, as is typical of Scripture, things of eternal significance are being said here that are true for all cultures and all times.

The eternal principle it teaches is this: It is our responsibility to notice the world around us and allow what we see to prompt questions about why it exists and what our part in it might be. We dare not:

- lazily shrug our shoulders, switch off our brain, and reach for another Chardonnay;

- protect ourselves from the uncomfortable possibility of God by grasping at poorly thought out philosophies and arguments;
- repress what we instinctively know to be true about God so that we kill off all knowledge of him;
- scorn the possibility of God so that we can pursue our chosen lifestyle.

These are responses for which God might reasonably hold us culpable. We may feel that his existence is an uncomfortable and inconvenient truth, but that of itself doesn't make it less true.

If God exists – and if he is who he has revealed himself to be in Scripture – then truth really does exist. Truth is not just a relative thing, something that "works for you" in the moment. If God exists, truth is what God defines it to be and guarantees it to be. The very quality of truth has to spring from the essence of who God is. The Bible reports that God is truthful (Psalm 119:160) and that his word can be trusted (Psalm 33:4).

However, while truth may exist, we always have the choice of whether or not to embrace it.

History teaches that strife inevitably occurs when God's truth is ignored. Despite strident objections from militant atheists, it really does seem to be the case that faithfulness to God, truth, and morality are linked (Isaiah 59:12–15; Jeremiah 7:28; 9:4–6). The converse is also true. Godlessness and the suppression of truth are often linked… and when this occurs, it can have devastating consequences for society.

The fact is, God places the highest priority on truth and expects us to be diligent and honest in seeking it out. His word in Scripture tells us to be "dressed" in truth (Ephesians 6:13–14) and that those who exhibit God's quality of love will "rejoice" in the truth (1 Corinthians 13:6).

God, of course, has given us complete freedom to seek out truth or not. Needless to say, his hope is that we will choose to reach for truth... and find him.

Dare to find meaning

Postmodernists say that moral and spiritual truth doesn't exist. They may allow that empirically defined truth exists in the realm of science, but truth does not exist when it comes to spiritual things. Spiritual truth has no more significance than the truth of you liking one particular flavour of ice cream more than another. Take your pick. Choose whatever works best for you in your current situation, and feel free to change your flavour next week.

I can't help feeling that this is a capitulation to laziness, meaninglessness, and despair. The particular flavour of ice cream that is God has done a fair bit to commend the truth of his existence. He comes wrapped in a universe of unimaginable wonder; he has given us "tasters" in coming to us personally as Jesus; he has even paid for the ice cream so you can experience it! These are non-trivial things that deserve our investigation.

I certainly don't want anyone to put their faith in anything that is not credible or deserving of them, which prompts the question: What good reasons are there that might make a person want to explore the veracity of faith?

I can think of ten. Here they are:

1. Faith has to be more than a philosophy. There need to be historical records of God invading human history in acts of self-revelation if it is claimed that God wants to interact with humans (Hebrews 1:1–2; 1 John 1:1).

2. Faith needs to be morally credible. God, by definition, cannot have a morality that is inferior to our own (Numbers 23:19; 1 Peter 1:15–16).

3. Faith has to be able to be understood by everyone, not just the academic or theological elite (Mark 10:15). Otherwise it will just be another form of man-made, elitist Gnosticism. (Gnostics believe that God is known by secret knowledge known only to a few.)

4. Faith must have withstood the test of time – time in which a corpus of truth has steadily built up and never contradicted itself (Matthew 5:17–18; 1 John 2:7).

5. Faith needs to be compatible with the truth seen in other disciplines, specifically science.[38] Different truths cannot war against each other if they all have the same divine origin.

6. Authentic faith needs the consistent testimony of people being changed by their belief so that they are more God-like. If the Christian God is true, this means being more:

   • joyful (even in affliction);

   • indiscriminate in love;

   • truthful.

In other words, it needs the testimony of being able to transform character (Romans 12:2; 2 Corinthians 3:18). Allied to this, authentic faith can be expected to show evidence of divine power.

7. The essential tenets of faith must be trans-cultural. The consistent principles of Scripture cannot be culturally imprisoned but must apply equally to all cultures and all periods of history (Galatians 3:28).

8. Faith needs to have a consistent anchor (or guardian) of its doctrine so that it is not distorted by the ungrounded

speculation or false claims of successive generations. In other words, it needs Scripture (Matthew 22:29; John 10:35; 2 Timothy 3:16).

9. Faith has to be relevant. It must have a reason for being, otherwise it is just a meaningless (or at best, temporary) exercise with no lasting goal or significance. In other words, it needs the goal of God's coming, eternal kingdom (Revelation 21:1–2).

10. Faith must make the most complete sense possible of the greatest conundrums regarding the human condition, namely sin and suffering (Luke 6:21; James 1:2–4; Revelation 21:4).

Christianity answers these requirements better than any other faith or philosophy I know.

Truth matters

Truth matters. Instinctively, we know this to be true. There is something good about truth. Truth seems to be something outside of us, beyond us – something that measures us and invites us to climb up to it. Most of us are glad that truth is there, even if we can't always reach it.

To act in a way that is true and right is to live out a concept of truth that is unique to humans. Simply to act in a way that is merely expedient or programmed by evolution is to be subhuman – to be less than we have been called to be. It is to collapse back into nature "red in tooth and claw" where it makes perfect sense to enslave, kill, and exploit others to ensure that we thrive.

Please don't be subhuman. There is good evidence that truth is very important.

Ask, seek, and knock

Jesus has given us an intriguing invitation. This invitation was given at a time when a great number of religions and philosophies were vying for people's allegiance. There were the Greco-Roman pantheon of gods from the north; the gods of Egypt (including Isis and Osiris) from the south; as well as the mystery religions from Asia in the east. The religious scene then was every bit as confusing as it is today. Jesus' invitation therefore has a huge relevance to all those who are seeking truth. Here is his invitation:

Ask and it will be given you, seek and you will find;
knock and the door will be opened to you. For everyone
who asks receives; the one who seeks finds: and to the
one who knocks, the door will be opened.

(Matthew 7:7–8)

In essence, this is an invitation for us to do some work – work that will result in us knowing and experiencing things we have never known before. Those who ask God for understanding; those who seek truth; and those who knock on his door – will find what they are looking for. God invites us to "do" what is necessary to know him and engage with him.

So, here's the question: How forcefully will you and I pursue knowing the truth about God?

Some notable atheists have dared to do so. They have had the courage to venture out from their ideological comfort zones and do some serious research into the life, death, and resurrection of Jesus. One of them was Josh McDowell, who went on to become a celebrated American apologist for the Christian gospel. Another was Albert Ross, author of the 1930 bestseller *Who Moved the Stone?*[39]

The twentieth-century British philosopher Anthony Flew was a strong advocate of atheism. Nonetheless, he was committed to following the path of evidence wherever it led when analysing religion. Doing so finally caused him to confess his belief in God. When explaining why he changed his mind, he said that his decision was in keeping with his lifelong Socratic commitment to go where the evidence leads.[40]

The evidence is there… if we want to find it.

Truth

If God exists, truth exists. And if truth exists, it calls for more than a mild nod of the head. The consequences of the existence of a God of truth are huge. C.S. Lewis put this well when he wrote:

> *One of the greatest difficulties is to keep before the audience's mind the question of Truth. They always think you are recommending Christianity not because it is true, but because it is good. And in the discussion they will at every moment try to escape from the issue "True or False" into stuff about a good society, or morals, or incomes of Bishops, or the Spanish inquisition… or anything whatever. You have to keep forcing them back, and again back, to the real point. Only thus you will be able to undermine their belief that a certain amount of "religion" is desirable but one mustn't carry it too far. One must keep on pointing out that Christianity is a statement which, if false, is of no importance, and if true, is of infinite importance. The one thing it cannot be is moderately important.[41]*

When exploring issues of truth, atheism does not do well. It is unable to give a credible explanation of an ordered universe or take adequate account of the historical Jesus. Not only that, but the lack of care shown with truth by many of atheism's leading exponents does little to commend it.

The one true God – who has revealed himself as Jesus Christ – loves truth, embodies truth, and *is* truth. That's why there is good reason to believe that if you search for truth, you will hear the whisper of God.

7

THE EVIDENCE OF GOD IN DEATH

There is something awfully final about death. After the miracle of birth, death seems a bit of an anticlimax. There is no fanfare, just the slow turning off of the switch for many of us. It's hardly the curtain call sought by most actors who "*strut and fret their hour upon the stage*".[1]

Any spiritual claim concerning humanity needs to make sense of both our beginning (why we exist) and our ending (why death exists). These two events peg out the limit of our existence and remind us that life is linear: it has a beginning and an end that are defined by time.

Death is certainly a mystery that has baffled humanity throughout history. Some of us dread it, a few of us welcome it… and all of us have to face it.

Here's my thesis: If God exists, then it's likely that evidence for his existence will be seen in this extraordinarily significant event. But if this evidence can be seen, what does it look like?

Let's explore.

Does it make sense logically and practically?

When Jesus was on planet Earth, he impacted people with two things. The first was his words, and the second was his actions. They went hand in hand – always. This gives us a model for exploring the evidence of God in death. First, let's look at the Bible's teaching on death to see whether it makes sense. Is it logically, morally, and experientially true (as far as we can judge)? If not, we need not concern ourselves with God any longer.

Second, let's look for evidence of God in the actions and events that occur at the point of death. Do people experience something significant at the moment of their transition between life and whatever comes next? If these experiences exist, what do they teach us? Do they suggest that death is a door or a wall? Is it an ending or an opportunity?

Death is an angst-ridden thing

The mystery of death has fuelled religions, rites, and superstitions throughout history. Human societies are either morbidly obsessed with it, or they hide from it and don't let their children see it; they speak of it in hushed tones and invent euphemisms such as "passed away" so that they won't have to say the "D" word.

Huge industries exist dedicated to delaying the symptoms of aging – signs that we are getting nearer to death. This betrays an unvoiced conviction within most human beings that our sense of worth is determined by our apparent fitness to mate. Death represents ultimate "unfitness" and is therefore to be postponed for as long as possible. If you can't stay young, at least look young.

Some industries hold out the hope that you might be able to cheat death altogether. They offer to freeze your body cryogenically at the point of death in the hope that future medical breakthroughs might mean your body can be thawed, resuscitated, and healed of sickness and aging. Others are less scrupulous. For a while, emails were buzzing about inviting us to send $200 and a lock of our hair so that our DNA could be stored in the hope that we could be reconstituted at some future point in history.

Whatever else people choose to believe about death, it's regarded as a big deal, something to be avoided. The urge to stay alive is driven by the basic instinct to propagate and thrive. Added to this is the reluctance we feel at losing the strong relationships we have developed – a sentiment well voiced by the Welsh poet Dylan Thomas, who exhorted his dying father to *"not go gentle into that good night"*, but to, *"rage, rage, against the dying of the light"*.[2]

The ancient Egyptians went to great lengths to ensure the survival of their souls after death. They provided tombs, grave goods, and offerings to preserve the bodies and spirits of the deceased so that they could journey safely and well to the afterlife.

In India, Mahatma Ghandi founded the Swaraj movement, a social and political movement that advocated self-rule and freedom from political overlords. Significantly, he did this not just to improve society, but to introduce a godly lifestyle that would give people the hope of reincarnation into a better life. His objective was to help people overcome their fear of death.[3]

We don't like death. Many people, such as the poet William Cary, have a fear of it. When he saw a canary singing happily in a cage, he thought gloomily that it could only do so because it didn't know it was going to die.

We have an innate instinct to survive for as long as possible. Interestingly enough, this instinct does not switch off once we have done our biological duty and our children have become adults. We do not then meekly surrender to death, calm in the knowledge that we have done our job. Instead, we become social burdens. In our aged state, we use up resources, clog up supermarket queues, and require more than our fair share of medical resources. Surely evolution should have taught us to get out of the way with the minimum of fuss as soon as our biological job was done! But it hasn't. We hang on to life as tenaciously as possible. We hate death because of its uncertainty and because it ruptures the bonds of love we have formed.

The big question is: Have we invented God simply to give us the illusion that there is meaning and hope after death – making the prospect of death more palatable? [4]

Fear of death certainly helps to focus people's attention on religion.[5] This is understandable. Research indicates that a person's commitment to religion generally lowers their fear of death.[6]

Clearly, if religion has no basis in truth, then an awful lot of people are mistaken. Could it be that they are all experiencing delusions of the mind as a result of puffing on Karl Marx's opium pipe? Or is it that they have caught a whiff of something true?

Has God left a clue about himself in the whole issue of death?

Take a look at the book

Pastors are familiar with funerals. They are bittersweet occasions that show up the whole muddle of the human condition. There are tears, fond memories, and lots of stories. Significantly, there is also a great deal of untruth and theological confusion. Funerals are times when people reach for the emotional analgesic of sentimentalism – which they mistake for spirituality. Clichés and platitudes are spoken to help people get through the funeral day, if not through life. Poems are read that say things like, "I'm not really dead; I am in the raindrop and the breeze" – an idea that has more in common with Buddhism than with Christianity. Or, "My beloved is now an angel in heaven." It's sweet, but utterly untrue.

Christianity, as defined by the New Testament, is unambiguous in insisting on the reality of the resurrection. The concept, which was fairly vague in Judaism, became clearly defined in

Christianity. The Christian church holds resurrection to be of central importance. The Anglican theologian Tom Wright says:

> *Take away the stories of Jesus' birth, and all you lose is*
> *two chapters in Matthew and two in Luke. Take away*
> *the resurrection and you lose the entire New Testament*
> *and most of the second-century fathers as well.*[7]

So, what does the Bible say?

Jesus spoke about the resurrection in Matthew 22:23–32. He made it clear that resurrected people will be *like* the angels but will not *be* angels; relationships will be taken to a whole new level in eternity, superseding even that of marriage. This passage also teaches that the resurrection is a future event, not something that happens in the instant a person dies.

The Apostle Paul stresses the central importance of the resurrection in 1 Corinthians 15, his most comprehensive teaching on the subject. He teaches that if Jesus had not been resurrected, but had simply disappeared into some sort of spiritual state, death would not have been defeated and we would have no hope of resurrection ourselves.[8]

In the same passage, Paul contrasts our current physical body with our resurrected spiritual body. When he says that our future body will be spiritual, he does not mean that it will be non-material. He means that it will be a body animated by a spiritually transformed soul, one that is no longer corrupted by sin. In other words, our resurrected body will not be a disembodied spiritual phantom; it will have a transformed physicality. Paul teaches in Philippians 3:20–21 that our resurrected body will be like Jesus' resurrected body. That is to say, it will be real but transformed so that it is different.

What, then, does Jesus' resurrection teach us about the central claims of Christianity?

While there are variations in the resurrection accounts of Jesus (as you would expect from different eyewitnesses to any incident), the following features are consistent:

1. The body of Jesus was missing from the tomb.

2. Women made the discovery that Jesus' body was missing. In the time of Jesus, women were considered to be unreliable witnesses, indicating that it is unlikely that this story was fabricated.

3. An angel told the disciples that Jesus had risen from the dead. What is clear in the resurrection accounts is that the disciples were not expecting Jesus to be resurrected. Nothing in Jewish tradition had prepared them for such an event, so they were every bit as sceptical about a resurrection claim as people would be today. Thomas, one of the disciples, illustrated this. It was not until he saw Jesus himself and felt the physical reality of his body that he believed (John 20:24–28). Jesus' resurrection compelled the disciples to face the fact that God was inaugurating a whole new creation from the seeds of the old creation.

A key teaching of the New Testament is that Jesus was the first one to be resurrected (the "first fruit") and that those who put their trust in him will, at some future date, be similarly resurrected. Jesus' rising from the dead meant that the resurrection process had begun… and that it will include everyone else when Jesus returns on the last day.

The festival of Passover commemorated God's saving grace in rescuing the Israelites from slavery in Egypt. The Israelites extended the meaning of the Passover, making it a time when they also thanked God for the "first fruits" of the wheat harvest. In his letter to the Corinthians, the Apostle Paul applies this first fruit imagery to Jesus. Jesus, who is God's saving grace towards us, is the "firstfruits" to rise from the dead (1 Corinthians 15:20). We will follow on later when Jesus comes again to wrap up this old, imperfect universe and inaugurate the kingdom of God.

So, what will this resurrected existence look like?

We get some good clues from three sources.

The first clue comes from Jesus' resurrected body. Fairly obviously, it is the model for the resurrected body for all of us. The Apostle John makes this clear when he says, "*We shall be like him*" (1 John 3:2).

The Bible tells us that Jesus' resurrected body was a physical body but it was different. It was not subject to all our current physical limitations (it could pass through doors), yet it could be touched and was able to eat food (Luke 24:36–43; John 20:19–20). As such, the resurrected body is not a ghost.

In Romans 8:23, Paul speaks of the "*redemption of our bodies*". This tells us that God's people are promised a new type of bodily existence. For some of us, that will be good news indeed!

The second clue about what the resurrection life will be like comes from the parable Jesus told about a rich man, and Lazarus (a beggar) who sat at his gate (Luke 16:19–31). In this story, we see that the things that frustrate the purposes of God from being fully realized in us will be transformed. After Lazarus died, he was restored and comforted in the care of Abraham. This suggests that all those who are resurrected will be free of the crippling circumstances of life and will realize their full potential in God's kingdom.

The Apostle Paul also taught this idea. He said that our physical body is like a seed, which, unless it dies, cannot grow to realize its full spiritual potential (1 Corinthians 15:37–38, 42–44). This, incidentally, may have implications for those who die young, perhaps even those who die before birth.

A pause for breath

It's worth pausing here and asking: Does this teaching make any sense? Does it contain any obvious signs of stupidity or folly? Bear in mind this is not mysticism; this is concrete teaching from historical human beings. Much of it comes from the mouth of Jesus. The question is: Does it stand up?

It certainly teaches that we are not free to treat God's creation with disdain; we are called to care for it because it will be used to seed the coming kingdom of God. This at least warrants a moral tick.

The biblical accounts of the resurrection of Jesus show the sort of miraculous hand that you could only expect if God existed. But, crucially, they also contain the earthy, historical details of a group of people who clearly didn't expect Jesus to be resurrected. In other words, it has the ring of historical authenticity.

Jesus' resurrection is not an easy thing to explain away. The resurrected Jesus wasn't a ghost; people touched him and ate with him.

He wasn't a fiction invented by the early disciples; they didn't expect him to be resurrected. When they encountered the resurrected Jesus, it transformed their ministry. It galvanized an evangelistic zeal and gave them a conviction for which they were prepared to die.

Jesus couldn't have simply fainted on the cross and then been resuscitated. He was crucified by Roman soldiers who also speared his chest, rupturing the pericardium around his heart. By any stretch of the imagination, he was dead!

Neither is it likely that the Roman authorities stole the body of Jesus. All they had to do to stop the infant Christian church from developing was produce Jesus' body – but they couldn't do so.

The resurrection accounts of Jesus are both historically reasonable and supernatural, as they would have to be if the biblical story of Christ were true.

It seems that God's fingerprints are all over the Bible's teaching about death. It is a teaching that gives us hope.

Heaven: what's it all about?

Is Jesus' teaching about heaven believable?

The Bible teaches that Christians who die go to a place where they wait until Christ comes again, at which point they will be resurrected. That "waiting place" is called heaven (or "paradise"). Jesus said:

> *My Father's house has many rooms; if that were not*
> *so, would I have told you that I am going there to*
> *prepare a place for you? And if I go and prepare a place*
> *for you, I will come back and take you to be with me*
> *that you also may be where I am.*

(John 14:2–3)

This passage does not mean that we will die and immediately go to our allotted "room", which Jesus has prepared for us in heaven. It means that Jesus is getting our place ready in his kingdom and he will, *at some future date*, come back to take us into it.

This understanding is supported by the conversation Jesus had with the repentant thief who was being crucified next to him (Luke 23:39–43). In this conversation, the thief asks Jesus to remember him when Jesus comes to his kingdom. Jesus says to him, "*Today you will be with me in paradise.*" In other words, the thief would be with Jesus in paradise before Jesus was even resurrected. As Jesus is the first to be resurrected, it follows that the thief could not be resurrected before Jesus. He would have to wait in "paradise", sometimes called "heaven", until Jesus was resurrected and came again to inaugurate God's new kingdom.

Our resurrected, kingdom state is something that is kept in heaven until it is ready for us to inherit. Peter writes:

> *Praise be to the God and Father of our Lord Jesus*
> *Christ! In his great mercy he has given us new birth*
> *into a living hope through the resurrection of Jesus*
> *Christ from the dead, and into an inheritance that can*
> *never perish, spoil or fade. This inheritance is kept in*
> *heaven for you...*
>
> (1 Peter 1:3–4)

So, even the dead who have been faithful to God have to wait. John writes in Revelation 6:10–11 of God's faithful people in heaven expressing their longing and asking Jesus how long it will be before he brings about his final judgment. Jesus gives them a white robe (symbolizing purity) and tells them to wait until the full number of those who will suffer for Christ is realized. In other words, those who are already dead are in heaven waiting for Jesus' second coming, at which point they will be resurrected, judged, and allocated their eternal inheritance.

The Greek word *parousia* (used to describe Jesus' second coming in 1 Thessalonians 4:15 and 1 Corinthians 15:23) is usually translated "coming", but it literally means "presence". It alludes to the idea that the absent but ruling Lord will one day appear and rule his kingdom in person.[9]

Judgment: not a nice idea!

The picture of Jesus coming as judge is a key aspect of his second coming (Romans 14:9–10; 2 Corinthians 5:10) but it's not an idea that always sits well with us. Judgment carries negative connotations. Jesus' judgment, however, will be positive in that injustice, suffering, and evil will finally be corrected. Without judgment, these things would remain wrong and unchallenged forever.

The Bible teaches that it is not just godly people who will be resurrected. Jesus spoke about both the righteous *and* the unrighteous being raised from the dead (John 5:28–29).

Similarly, it is not just unfaithful people who will be judged. Everyone will be judged, whether they are living or dead (John 5:28–29; Acts 10:42; Hebrews 9:27). Those who have not chosen to accept God's love will have their decision honoured and will not have any future with God. For them, only the second death awaits (Revelation 20:6). Those who *have* accepted God's love will also be judged in order to determine the level of their reward for their faithfulness on Earth (Mark 9:41; Matthew 16:27; 25:34–36; Ephesians 6:8; Hebrews 11:26). Then they will be invited to live eternally in God's new kingdom.

There is beautiful justice in this.

Hell: a culturally irrelevant idea… isn't it?

Let's admit it, it is not popular to talk about hell. Some dismiss the idea as an archaic theological concept drawn from ancient, culturally imprisoned writings.

There is some truth in this. The Bible does reflect the culture of the time in which it was written. However, we are required by God to see through the Bible's cultural context to the consistent principles that God has placed in Scripture for the benefit of all people in all ages. The question is this: Is the concept of hell just a cultural gloss, or is it core Christian teaching? Does hell exist?

Let's explore.

Christian teaching makes two things clear. The first is that God is loving. In fact, God is the most perfect definition of love. The second is that God is just. He is the most perfect definition of justice. It is important to understand that these two defining characteristics of God are not in tension. They don't cancel each other out in order to make room for each other in God's essential nature. Both exist fully and perfectly in God.

God's holiness and justice mean that he has zero tolerance for evil. Evil is not something that God can overlook or accommodate because it directly challenges his holiness. Therefore, God will (and must) destroy evil utterly and completely. God does this by killing it off. The story of Adam and Eve teaches us that death was the consequence of Adam and Eve's rebellion against God. Death means that human sinfulness cannot live forever. It is God's judgment on sin. Those with any trace of sin in them are condemned by God's judgment to face death (Romans 6:23).

The good news, however, is that God has chosen to rescue people back into his kingdom by sending Jesus to die for our sins, so that we can be eligible for eternal life with God. His motive for doing this was love. All we have to do is receive God's love, accept Jesus' death on our behalf, and let God be Lord of our lives.

The gospel (which literally means "good news") is all about triumphing over death (Revelation 2:11). Jesus said: "*Whoever hears my word and believes him who sent me has eternal life and will not be judged but has crossed over from death to life*" (John 5:24).

Some have claimed that since God created everything, he must be responsible for the existence of sin and death… so it's all his fault. This is not so. Sin and death are not things that God caused to exist. They are caused by the absence of God in the same way that cold is caused by the absence of heat. Where God is, sin and death cannot exist.

What happens to those who die?

When those who are faithful to God die, their final judgment is anticipated by the fact that they go to heaven (or paradise). This is a glorious place where they wait for Jesus to join a new heaven with a totally transformed Earth and begin his eternal kingdom. When Jesus comes again to do this, both the living and the dead will be resurrected. Then they will be judged, rewarded, and invited to take their place in God's kingdom.

Those who have chosen to reject God's lordship follow a similar pathway, albeit one with a very different outcome. Their eternal status after death is anticipated by the fact that they are being sent to a place of punishment (2 Peter 2:9), sometimes called "Hades" (Revelation 20:13). When Jesus comes again, they will be resurrected, judged, and required to face the final consequence. This event is referred to in the Bible as the "second death" (Revelation 20:6).

Christians are divided as to what the "second death" actually is. Some think the ungodly are finally annihilated, while others think there is some form of eternal punishment. Whatever it is, it must be consistent with the just and compassionate nature of God.

The idea that the ungodly are annihilated is consistent with the notion of there being a "second death". It is also consistent with the Scriptures, which teach that evil will be completely destroyed (2 Peter 3:7; Matthew 10:28). However, believing that the ungodly will be annihilated requires you to treat the language of eternal torment in Scripture as metaphorical (Matthew 25:46; Luke 16:22–23; Revelation 14:11; 20:10–15). It means understanding eternal absence from God (because of annihilation) as eternal torment. Certainly, it is eternally significant!

When talking about God's judgment, it is important to remember that God's agenda is for us to be saved, not sent to hell. God did not intend anyone to go to hell (1 Thessalonians 5:9). The very reason Jesus came was to stop that happening. Hell was designed primarily for the Devil and his evil spirits, who are the antithesis of God (Matthew 25:41). For people to go to hell, they will need to have rejected God's will for them (2 Peter 3:9). We must understand that God will respect anyone's decision to have nothing to do with him – both now and in eternity. C.S. Lewis has suggested that "*the gates of hell are locked from the inside*".[10] This may be going too far, but it does suggest that hell is a chosen state – one that we choose while living on Earth.

Reviewing God's report card

Well, how is God doing? Is God a god of compromise; one who allows those who are 49 per cent sinful into heaven? Does he simply require our good deeds to outweigh our bad deeds?

No. God has zero tolerance for evil: he has to if he is to remain holy.

However, does this mean that God will judge and destroy all of humanity because none of us are perfect?

No, it doesn't. He came to us as Jesus Christ to pay the price for our sins and rescue us back to himself.

This beautiful interplay of love and holiness gets a huge moral tick from us. Something deep within us sighs and says, "That feels right."

But that doesn't let God off the hook. Two other issues surrounding death need to be explored. The first concerns the status of those who have never heard about Jesus. Is the Christian teaching about this fair? The second is closely related: Has God predestined some to go to heaven and others to go to hell? For if God has predestined some to go to hell, then that is unfair. As the morality of such a God is inferior to *our* morality, God can be dismissed as a rather bad human invention.

What about other faiths?

What does God want us to believe about other faiths? How are we to account for the reforming zeal of Mohandas Gandhi, the compassion of Buddha, and the wisdom of Confucius?

The Christian gospel makes it plain that people are not made acceptable to God by their moral leadership, their insight, or their piety. While these things can be commendable and good, they don't earn us God's acceptance. If God is to remain holy, his standard is absolute *perfection* – a standard that none of us can attain. That's why God came to us as Jesus to die on a cross, paying the price for our sins so that we could have free access to God. It was an act of love that God freely chose. We are invited to respond by accepting God's love, putting our faith in what Jesus did on our behalf, and beginning to live for God's purposes.

But this leaves us with a dilemma. By saying that Christ's death on the cross is indispensable for the salvation of the world, we appear to be condemning other faiths as inadequate. Yet if we say that other ways to God are equally valid, the cost of this is to give up Christ as the only one who can rescue humankind back to God.

There are three possible positions that we could take:

Pluralism: There are many ways to God

The first position is that of "pluralism". Pluralists find it objectionable to think that only those who acknowledge the "Christian God" will be saved. Accordingly, they teach that all religions lead to God.

There are two main types of pluralism. The first of these is "ethical pluralism". This says that only those religions that are good, that care for the poor and insist on justice, are valid. (This, of course, raises the interesting question of who decides what "good" is.)

Some feminists support this position because, in their view, insisting that only one religion is right has clear parallels to sexism (it's like saying that one gender is superior). They say that "justice" is the fundamental value of religion and should be religion's central focus.

Another form of pluralism suggests that all religious experiences are encounters with the same God. The various religions are culturally and historically conditioned human responses to a sense of the divine that is beyond us.

The problem with pluralism, however, is that it is very obviously a human construct – something that human beings have invented. God has not contributed anything to it at all.

It is significant that this idea of God is popular with Deists, who deny that God has any personal involvement with humanity. Deism is simply moralism dressed up in religious clothes, and it fails to address some vital issues. Humanity's inherent sinfulness is not dealt with; nothing is said about life after death; ultimate justice is not guaranteed; and God remains perverse and unknowable, hiding behind the contradictory and changing images of a thousand different religions.

Sadly, there are many Deists within the institutional Christian church, more than a few in senior positions. Some of them are lovely people. They call themselves "liberal Christians". This means that they have largely dispensed with everything that is diagnostic about Christianity – for example, Christ's saving action on the cross and his resurrection. Fundamentally, they have reduced Christianity to moralism.

Conventional, biblical Christianity, however, is a completely different religion. It teaches that God has chosen to come to us as Jesus Christ to show us the essence of himself. It teaches that he came to show us how to live sacrificial lives of integrity and love, and above all, that he came to die in order to win us back to God.

Christianity cannot be reduced to a moral philosophy that tells us how we should live. Jesus' claims are too exclusive. He claimed to be the same as God; he accepted worship; he forgave sins; he said he was the only way to God; he claimed that his death would rescue humanity back to God... and he claimed to have been resurrected from the dead as an indication that all this was true. Jesus' death and resurrection are therefore not optional garnishes to Christianity; they *define* Christianity.

Exclusivism: There is only one way to God

The second position that can be held concerning who makes it to heaven is exclusivism. Exclusivists believe that those who have not heard the gospel or who belong to other faiths cannot be saved.

However, this contradicts God's expressed will that *everyone* should be saved (1 Thessalonians 5:9; 2 Peter 3:9). It also contradicts the three things we know about God's character: that God is righteous (Psalms 19:9; 145:17); that God is love (1 John 4:7–10, 16); and that God is just (Psalm 89:14; Revelation 16:7).

The justice of God is shown in the biblical passages that teach that God will take into account what we know when judging us (Luke 12:47–48; 1 Timothy 1:13). They teach that God will judge us according to two things: how we have responded to Jesus (John 3:36; Hebrews 10:29) and how we have responded to our conscience – the ethical laws we instinctively know to be right (Romans 2:14–16). This is significant because, while not everyone has the opportunity to respond to Jesus, everyone has the opportunity to faithfully live out the values they know to be right.

The Bible teaches us that the incredible wonder and complexity of the universe should point people to the possibility that God exists (Psalm 19:1–4; Romans 1:19–20). As such, it is reasonable for people to seek God and live life as well as they can in the light of God's existence. It is also reasonable to agree with the Bible's judgment that where people persistently rebel against what they know to be good, there is no possibility of a relationship with God. A certain humility of heart is needed if one is to acknowledge God, and not everyone has this. God gives all people the ability to perceive him, but not everyone chooses to use this gift.

So, if neither pluralism nor exclusivism is right, what *is* right?

Inclusivism – with a twist

A third position that can be adopted is inclusivism. This maintains the central claims of Christianity but adopts a more positive view of other religions. Inclusivists hold Jesus to be unique and essential, but they believe that God is revealing himself and providing salvation through other religious traditions as well.

On the surface, this position sounds reasonable; however, it is dangerous. Its danger comes from what is meant by salvation of people "through" other faith positions, for the Bible makes it clear that salvation comes *only* through Jesus. The Apostle Peter said, "*Salvation is found in no one else, for there is no other name under heaven given to mankind by which we must be saved*" (Acts 4:12).

The inclusivist position therefore needs to be modified slightly so that biblical truth is more faithfully represented.

Modified inclusivism allows that there is undeniable truth and beauty in some other religions. However, these truths do not add anything new to the essentials of salvation as revealed in the Bible. It is not that people can be saved *through* other religions so much as they, by God's grace, may have access to Christ's saving act *from* their own sincerely held faith position.

To conclude this section, it is worth noting that God's attitude to those from other faith positions is clearly seen in his choice to announce the birth of Jesus to a bunch of New Age-style astrologers, most likely Zoroastrians from Persia. By doing this, God sent a clear signal that Jesus was his gift to people of all faiths and nations... and that all honest seekers will find him.

I submit that this shows the goodness and justice of God.

Has God predestined some people to go to hell?

Has God created some people with the intention that they will end up in hell? The idea that God could do such a thing is not at all nice!

It's worth treading a little carefully here as it is the nature of evil to ascribe evil to God (in order to tear God down), and, perversely, to elevate evil so that it appears good. So, let's agree not to go there.

The question of whether God has made some people to go to hell is a valid one, as many writings, particularly from the

Apostle Paul, suggest that God has already chosen those who will be saved to live eternally with him in his new kingdom. Here are a few verses that might indicate that this is the case:

> *For those God foreknew he also predestined to be conformed to the image of his Son, that he might be the firstborn among many brothers and sisters. And those he predestined, he also called...*
>
> (Romans 8:29–30)

> *Therefore God has mercy on whom he wants to have mercy, and he hardens whom he wants to harden.*
>
> (Romans 9:18)

> *For he chose us in him before the creation of the world to be holy and blameless in his sight. In love he predestined us for adoption to sonship through Jesus Christ...*
>
> (Ephesians 1:4–5)

> *Therefore, as God's chosen people, holy and dearly loved...*
>
> (Colossians 3:12)

> *For we know, brothers and sisters loved by God, that he has chosen you...*
>
> (1 Thessalonians 1:4)

> *But we ought always to thank God for you, brothers and sisters loved by the Lord, because God chose you as firstfruits to be saved through the sanctifying work of the Spirit and through belief in the truth.*
>
> (2 Thessalonians 2:13)

So, how do we reconcile these verses with those which speak of God wanting everyone to be saved?

The answer is relatively straightforward, but one that is often missed, even by some theologians. It lies in the nature of God. The fact is, as we've often said in this book, God stands outside of time. The past, present, and future are equally clear to him. God therefore knows exactly who will respond to his invitation of love, and who will not... even though those who are making the decision have free choice.

It is probable that the Apostle Paul knew this, because he was able to speak of those who are predestined to be saved... and yet also speak of his own sense of urgency in preaching the gospel. Listen to his passion:

> *How, then, can they call on the one they have not believed in? And how can they believe in the one of whom they have not heard? And how can they hear without someone preaching to them?*
>
> (Romans 10:14)

In his first letter to the Corinthian church, he says, "*Woe to me if I do not preach the gospel!*" (1 Corinthians 9:16).

Paul wanted to tell people about Jesus so that they might be able to make a choice. The importance of our having free choice is something God insists on, and for very good reason: all authentic, loving relationships are entered into by choice. Love cannot be compelled or programmed. The primacy of free choice is insisted on consistently in Scripture (emphases mine):

> **Whoever** *believes and is baptized will be saved, but* **whoever** *does not believe will be condemned.*
>
> (Mark 16:16)

225

The Son of Man must be lifted up, that **everyone**
who believes may have eternal life in him. For God
so loved the world that he gave his one and only Son,
that **whoever** *believes in him shall not perish but have*
eternal life.

(John 3:14–16)

I am the gate; **whoever** *enters through me will be*
saved.

(John 10:9)

And **everyone** *who calls on the name of the Lord will*
be saved.

(Acts 2:21)

I am not ashamed of the gospel, because it is the power
of God that brings salvation to **everyone** *who believes.*

(Romans 1:16)

While only Jesus provides the means for us to have a relationship with God, such a relationship still requires the two agents involved to agree to the relationship. Here's an image which might help you to visualize how both free will and predestination work:

Picture yourself walking towards the gate by which people enter into heaven. As you approach this gate, you see written above it, "FREE WILL. ENTER ALL WHO CHOOSE TO." You decide to walk through the gate and enter into heaven, but on looking back, you see written above the gate, "PREDESTINED. YOU HAVE NOT CHOSEN ME; I HAVE CHOSEN YOU."

Rising beasts or fallen people?

Having examined the moral justice of God as the one who gives hope after death, let's now look at death itself.

Is death a necessary agent that allows sophisticated beasts to rise from the primordial swamp, or is death the consequence of human sinfulness, as Genesis 3 suggests? In other words, are we rising beasts or fallen people?[11]

There's no doubt about it: death is a handy thing. It allows the evolutionary process to happen. Death clears the stage of old organisms and makes space for new organisms to develop. The death of species less suited to an ecological niche allows better adapted species to thrive. This process of selection drives the engine of biological adaptation and diversity. It has resulted in you.

However, we still find it difficult to pump our fists in the air and yell, "Yay, fantastic! Isn't death terrific?" There is something in us that laments death and thinks of it as not a good thing. The question is: Does our aversion to death come from a desire, selected by evolution, to stay alive for as long as possible so that we can pass on our genetic information, or does it have a deeper cause?

The fact is, while death may be biologically useful for a species, it also represents the rupturing and ending of something we hold very dear: relationships. That's why we don't like it.

Perhaps this is a clue to understanding something more about the significance of death?

Certainly, the obscenity of death is the fact that it ruptures relationships. This is entirely consistent with Scripture. Death was the agent God used to sever his relationship with sin-corrupted humanity. It was the agent that ensured sin would be killed off and would not last forever. Death clears the stage of evil, just as it clears the stage of unfit species. Both theology and science speak a similar language at this point.

Could it be that there is room for both a theological and biological understanding of death?

Death is a necessary agent that allows biological diversity, but it is a horrible thing that reflects an imperfect creation, one spoiled by sin and suffering. As such, the sad reality of death points to the hope that God will one day end this corrupted creation and make all things new.

The end of our theological investigation

This is the end of our theological investigation into whether we can see evidence of God in death. I hope you will agree that God's teaching about death makes sense: it is both good and just. Rather wonderfully, biblical teaching not only makes sense of death; it gives us a hope that *transcends* death.

Now, let's ask if we can also see the presence of God in the physical act of dying. Has God left clues there for those who seek them? If such clues do exist, we would expect on the basis of God's character that they would not compel belief but invite belief. God always preserves the need for faith.

So, do any faint clues exist? And do we see them in the "near death experiences" (NDEs) many people have encountered?

Death and near death experiences

Here are a few stories. They are reliable. I say this because, sadly, some ideologically driven people are prone to colouring the truth for their own ends. But these stories are ones in which I have been personally involved, or which have been reported to me by honest people of good character – friends I know well, many of whom have distinguished careers in their academic field. They are not "nuts".

Neither am I a "nut". My first two degrees were in science and I have been a research scientist for twelve years. Truth matters to me. I am naturally sceptical until I see evidence. This, of course, doesn't make me infallible! But it does mean I'm cautious.

Let me tell you about Effie.

Effie was an elderly woman with a beautiful, doll-like face and dancing blue eyes. Tragically, a stroke had taken away her ability to speak. Another stroke then disfigured her pretty face and put her into hospital. Effie had a doting husband, Stan, who would ride his bike to the hospital each day in the months before she died. When Effie's end drew near, I sat with the two of them and read aloud Psalm 23, Effie's favourite. Then, the most extraordinary thing happened: Effie looked past me to the end of her bed and smiled as if recognizing someone. Her face came back to normal, a tear rolled down her face… and then she died, with every appearance of peace.

Here's another story.

I used to go to the retirement village next to the hospital to visit an old man. He was in his early nineties and had one of the gentlest natures of anyone I'd ever met. As a twelve-year-old boy, he'd been sent into the bushland west of the town with a flock of sheep for two years to avoid a deadly outbreak of some disease that had overtaken his parents' farm. (It's difficult to imagine any twelve-year-old doing the same thing today!) In his old age, the man's health deteriorated to the point where he had needed to be moved to the hospital. Sadly, when I visited him some days later, I discovered that he'd died during the night. The nurses who were on duty when he died were still there and they asked to speak with me. They reported that as he was about to die, he had looked past them and said, "Who is that man at the foot of my bed?"

"There's no one there," they had replied.

"But there is," he had insisted. "Can't you see? Who is he?"

"There's no one there."

The nurses said that their patient had been polite but insistent... and not in any way distressed.

What had he seen?

I don't know.

All I could do was chat with the nursing staff and encourage them not to be surprised by such things. It is best to allow the perceptions of those who are dying rather than deny them.

These are just some of the things that pastors are privileged to experience from time to time.

My friend, Richard Banham, was a pastor in a small country town in the Australian bush. On the day before he left to go on holiday, a mother in the community lost her baby boy during childbirth. Richard returned from his holiday to discover that the matron of the hospital had deemed the event to have been a stillbirth and had organized for the baby to be buried without ceremony beside the golf course. For many months thereafter, the child's parents were unable to move on from the grief and anger they felt over the handling of their stillborn child. Richard organized a memorial service to be conducted at the burial site. During the service, a song was played that was particularly significant for the parents. As the mother listened to the song, she had a vision of a blonde-haired boy in a blue tracksuit in the arms of Jesus. It was a powerful and distinct image. She wrestled with whether or not to tell her husband, for she thought it was simply the product of her distraught state. That night, however, as they lay in bed together, she decided to share what she'd experienced. She began to recount her vision, and then her husband interrupted her. "I know what you saw," he said. "You saw our son as a young boy with blonde hair, dressed in a blue tracksuit, in the arms of Jesus."

I can't explain this, but I can say it was a great comfort to the parents.

Dr Darryl Cross, a South Australian psychologist, shared with me two stories of clients with whom he was involved as a trauma counsellor. The first concerned a TV reporter named David Kellett. He was in a medically induced coma because of injuries sustained as a result of being knocked off his pushbike by a drunk driver. The doctors only gave him a 5 per cent chance of living because of the critically high level of pressure on his brain.

Two days after the accident, David's wife left the hospital to spend the night at a friend's home. While she was asleep, she heard David call out to her using the nickname he always reserved for her. She dismissed it, putting the experience down to her grief and distress. However, David was insistent. Eventually, she agreed to engage with the voice. David told her that it was all too hard; he was tired and wanted to go. His wife pleaded with him to remember the love he had for her and the children. The discourse went back and forth until David said he would "try".

Next morning, David's wife went to the hospital and discovered that the pressure on David's brain had dropped suddenly and remarkably. When she asked what time the change had occurred, they were able to tell her it had happened during the night at precisely the time when David had promised he would try.

The second experience Darryl shared concerned a man who had been severely injured as a result of a stack of pallets falling on top of him when he was walking beside a warehouse. He was taken to the Royal Adelaide Hospital (in South Australia). The man reported having an out-of-body experience in which he floated above the ambulance and watched it weave through traffic along North Terrace, sometimes driving on the wrong side of the road. He had a similar experience while he was being "worked on" inside a curtained cubicle of Accident and Emergency. He floated above the cubicle and was able to see into the curtained cubicles along from his. One of them contained a little boy.

Some time later, the man visited the Emergency Department while going to the hospital for rehabilitation. He asked the Director of Nursing if the little boy in the third cubicle away from him had survived. The records were checked and he was told that the boy had made a good recovery. However, the Director of Nursing was puzzled as to how he could have known about the boy, since he'd been unconscious all the time. When the man explained what had happened to him and what he had seen, the Director of Nursing was amazed.

What usually happens in a near death experience?

Research into NDEs is notoriously difficult to do. Too often, there is little to go on other than anecdotes and people's interpreted experiences. This has resulted in this area being bedevilled by exaggerated claims, or interpreted claims, by those with a philosophical barrow to push. So, what can we say?

An NDE is sometimes reported by an individual who has been clinically dead for a few minutes before being resuscitated. Evidently, about 18 per cent of patients experiencing cardiac arrest report having such an experience.

NDEs are not a recent phenomenon. They have been written about ever since the *Myth of Er* was penned to conclude *Plato's Republic* in the fourth century BC – and they have been reported in most cultures.

While there is a fair diversity in what is experienced in an NDE, there are some features that are regularly reported. What are they?

Typically, there is an awareness of being physically dead, yet having a sense of peace and wellbeing. Quite often, there is an out-of-body experience in which the person observes themselves from a distance, usually from above. Some report seeing things they couldn't have known unless they had witnessed them from an out-of-body perspective. A year-long study of heart attack survivors in the cardiac unit of Southampton General Hospital was headed by one of Britain's leading neuropsychiatrists, Dr Peter Fenwick. He said during a TV interview, *"There is now a wealth of evidence showing that people seem to be able to get information that they couldn't have got just lying unconscious on the floor."*[12]

It is not uncommon for patients to speak of moving along a pathway or tunnel towards an intensely bright, but not harsh, light. There is often some communication with someone at the source of the light. Other ethereal beings are sometimes present. People also speak of meeting loved ones who have died earlier. The experiences are invariably intense and detailed in nature. There is no sense of drowsiness or of being half-conscious.

NDEs do occasionally include distressing scenes. However, they are usually positive experiences. They typically result in the subject being much less frightened of death. In fact, many people who have had an NDE report great reluctance at having to return to life on Earth; they would rather stay in their NDE state.

A lot of research has been done over the years on NDEs. The Dutch cardiologist Pim van Lommel studied 344 patients who recovered from cardiac arrest. Sixty-two of these experienced some sort of NDE despite being clinically dead with flat-lined brainstem activity. As a result of his work, van Lommel was convinced that consciousness could continue despite a lack of neuronal activity in the brain. In a paper submitted to *The Lancet*, he and his fellow researchers said:

> *Our results show that medical factors cannot account for occurrence of NDE; although all patients had been clinically dead, most did not have NDE... If purely physiological factors caused NDE, most of our patients should have had this experience.*[13]

This is an extraordinary statement. It is saying that NDEs cannot be explained physiologically... and that leaves us with an intriguing mystery!

The results of an eighteen-month pilot study into NDEs were sufficiently encouraging to trigger a massive research programme into the NDEs of 2,060 heart attack patients in fifteen hospitals throughout the United Kingdom, United States, and Austria. The study, commenced in 2008 and concluded in 2014, was co-ordinated by Dr Sam Parnia at Southampton University.

Of the 2,060 cardiac arrest patients studied, 330 survived, 140 of whom were surveyed. Thirty-nine per cent of these said they had experienced some kind of awareness while being resuscitated.

The study concluded that memories of an out-of-body experience corresponded with actual events in 2 per cent of those who were aware of something after death. In one case, awareness was known to have occurred during a three-minute period when there was no heartbeat – even though the brain typically ceases to function within thirty seconds of the heart stopping.

The researchers concluded that these findings suggest more research needs to be done, as there is a good deal of imprecision surrounding terms currently used to describe the experience of death.

So, at this stage, we can do little more than guess at the factors that determine the existence and nature of an NDE. For what it's worth, here's my guess:

The factors that may determine what is experienced in an NDE

The potential near death
experience

Filter 1
Circumstances of death
(is it lingering or instant?)

Filter 2
Cultural predisposition
(including learned spiritual influences
and convictions… or lack of)

Filter 3
Connectedness with a "higher being"
(note: this may not correlate with "being
religious", as some religious people are
disconnected from God)

Filter 4
Connectedness and empathy
with others in life

The actual near death
experience
(or lack thereof)

Remember, however, the ability to recall an NDE may be affected by medication.

What's the significance of it?

There is no God. Kerry said so.

The Australian media mogul Kerry Packer had a heart attack in 1990 and was clinically dead for six minutes. He was reported to have said afterwards at a press conference:

> *I've been to the other side and let me tell you, son, there's [expletive] nothing there... there's no one waiting there for you, there's no one to judge you, so you can do what you [expletive] well like.*

He died fifteen years later, aged sixty-five.

The fact that only 18 per cent of those who briefly die experience an NDE didn't stop Kerry from making this theological pronouncement on behalf of everyone. His comment does, however, raise an interesting question: Why do some people experience an NDE and not others?

I don't think anyone knows.

The fact is, however, some people do indisputably have a near death experience. This prompts us to ask, Is this significant? Can we see evidence of God in an NDE?

Great care needs to be taken not to make exaggerated claims. However, the fact that NDEs happen so often and in a similar manner means that two things might reasonably be said:

1. If God exists and has left clues about his nature for us to find, then NDEs are entirely consistent with his existence. NDEs do not compel faith, but they certainly invite it. They are often transformative experiences that inspire those who experience them to live a more godly lifestyle.

2. NDEs point to the possibility that your essential identity is not just defined by a mechanical brain. You can experience things when electrical activity in your brain has flat-lined. It would seem that your brain is not the same as your mind and neural physics is not the same as personhood. Your soul can exist independently of your body.

Now that's food for thought!

It certainly provokes some very deep questions, such as: If your mind/personhood/soul exists outside your body, who are you? Could you be someone God chooses to love, and with whom he wants to share the adventure of eternity? Could it be that the essential you is someone God has caused to exist so that he can invite you to live with him forever in his kingdom?

Jesus' resurrection certainly gives us that hope. The fact that he overcame death (and was not just resuscitated) is the essential "show and tell" of Christianity. It is the proof God chose to give humanity to show that hope in the face of death is possible. Christ now invites us to live for him and in him so that we too can share in his resurrection (Romans 6:4–10). This hope caused the Apostle Paul to say triumphantly, "*Where, O death, is your sting?*" (1 Corinthians 15:55), The power of death has been consummately defeated.

The effect of this conviction on people who were dying was noted by the physician who attended Charles Wesley. The doctor had watched a number of Methodists die over the years and was moved to say, "*Most people die for fear of dying; but I never met with people such as yours. They are none of them afraid of death but are calm and patient... and resigned to the last.*" This led Charles's brother John Wesley to state, "*Our people die well.*"[14]

My hope is that you will be able to do so as well.

May I suggest that it is reasonable to conclude that the presence of God can be seen in death – and that this invites a response?

Now here's the big question: Where do we go from here? What do we do with all the things that have been learned?

If you have heard the whisper of God inviting you into a loving relationship with him, then do respond. Chat with him in prayer. Tell God that you accept Christ's sacrifice on your behalf… and that you want to live for his purposes.

Inherit the eternal future you were created for.

NOTES

Introduction

1. Plato was a Greek philosopher who lived about 400 BC.

2. C.G. Jung, *Modern Man in Search of a Soul*.

3. H.L. Mencken, *Minority Report*.

1 The Evidence of God in the Cosmos

1. Einstein delivered this quote at a symposium on science, philosophy, and religion in 1941. It was also published in *Nature*, 146 (1941), p. 605.

2. S. Hawking, *A Brief History of Time*, p. 1.

3. P. Davies, "Taking Science on Faith".

4. F. Hoyle, "Hoyle on Evolution", p. 105.

5. F. Hoyle, "The Universe: Past and Present Reflections", p. 16.

6. S. Hawking quoted in J. Boslough, *Stephen Hawking's Universe*, p. 30.

7. S.J. Gould, *Dinosaur in a Haystack: Reflections in Natural History*. The text is taken from his "Introduction".

8. P. Davies, *The Mind of God: Science and the Search for Ultimate Meaning*, p. 232.

9. S. Weinberg, *The First Three Minutes*, p. 154.

10. F. Dyson, *Infinite in all Directions*, pp. 117–18.

11. *Ibid.*, p. 249.

12. Terry Pratchett, *Lords and Ladies*.

13. L.R. Graham, *Science and Philosophy in the Soviet Union*, p. 173.

14. A. Linde, "The Self-Reproducing Inflationary Universe".

15. P. Davies, "Taking Science on Faith".

16. *Ibid.*

17. R.J. Russell, "Intelligent Life in the Universe: Philosophical and Theological issues" (working draft), Center for Theology and the Natural Sciences, Berkeley, USA. Available at http://www.ictp.trieste.it/~chelaf/

lecture.html. Robert Russell is director of the Center for Theology and Natural Sciences in Berkeley.

18. D. Wilkinson, *Christian Eschatology and the Physical Universe*, p. 21.

19. P. Davies, *How to Build a Time Machine*, p. 48.

20. B. Russell, *Why I Am Not a Christian and Other Essays on Religion and Related Subjects*, p. 107.

21. J. Polkinghorne, *Quarks, Chaos and Christianity*, p. 30.

22. C.S. Lewis, *Miracles: A Preliminary Study*, p. 63.

23. S. Hawking, *A Brief History of Time: From the Big Bang to Black Holes*, p. 291.

2 The Evidence of God in Nature

1. Bill Bryson, *A Short History of Nearly Everything*, p. 254.

2. Augustine, *Confessions*, X.29.

3. Translated from a Latin note written in the margin of Luther's Bible next to Romans 1:20. See: M. Luther, *Werke* (Weimarer Ausgabe: 1927), Vol. 48, p. 201. (Volume 48 has not yet been translated into English.)

4. J. Calvin, *Confessio Belgica* (1561), cited in A.E. McGrath, *Science and Religion: An Introduction*, p. 11.

5. Augustine, *De Genesi ad litteram*, II.9, I.21, trans. E. McMullin, "How Should Cosmology Relate to Theology?" in A.R. Peacocke (ed.), *The Sciences and Theology in the Twentieth Century*, pp. 17–57 (pp. 19, 20).

6. J. Calvin, *Commentaries: Genesis*, Vol. I, Genesis, chapter 1, verse 6, p. 79.

7. F. Bacon, *The Advancement of Learning*, 8 (1.1.3).

8. T. Browne, *Relgio Medici*, part I, section 16, pp. 18–19.

9. R. Boyle, *The Excellency of Theology Compared with Natural Theology* (tract, 1772) in R. Boyle, *The Works of the Honourable Robert Boyle*, Vol. 4, pp. 1–66.

10. I. Newton, "First Letter to Richard Bentley", p. 46.

11. Charles Darwin in a letter first published in 1887 by his son Francis

Darwin (F. Darwin [ed.], *The Life and Letters of Charles Darwin*, Vol. 1, p. 304).

12. F. Darwin, *The Life and Letters of Charles Darwin*, Vol. 2, p. 82.

13. F. Temple, "The Present Relations of Science to Religion": A sermon preached on 1 July 1860 before the University of Oxford. See: J. Brooke and G. Cantor, *Reconstructing Nature: The Engagement of Science and Religion*, p. 36.

14. C. Darwin, *The Autobiography of Charles Darwin*, p. 57.

15. A. Desmond and J. Moore, *Darwin*, p. 488.

16. J. Monod, *Chance and Necessity*, p. 167.

17. Francis Collins in an interview with CNN on 3 April 2007. See also his book: *The Language of God: A Scientist Presents Evidence for Belief.*

18. J. Polkinghorne, *Quarks, Chaos and Christianity*, pp. 42–49.

19. C. De Duve, "Lessons of Life", pp. 10–11.

20. S.W. Fox and K. Dose, *Molecular Evolution and the Origin of Life.*

21. C. De Duve, "Lessons of Life", pp. 6–8.

22. S.J. Gould, *Ever Since Darwin*, p. 104.

23. F. Watts (ed.), *Science Meets Faith: Theology and Science in Conversation*, p. 13.

24. R. Jastrow, *God and the Astronomers*, p. 116.

25. I. Tattersall, *Becoming Human: Evolution and Human Uniqueness.*

3 The Evidence of God in Suffering

1. N.J. Hawkes, "An Apology for the Scientific Credibility of Faith" (Sydney: Australian College of Theology, doctoral thesis, 2004), pp. 124–25.

2. V.E. Frankl, *Man's Search for Meaning*, pp. 178–83.

3. See Job 1:8–12; 2:3–6; Ephesians 3:10; 6:12.

4. A.R. Peacocke, *Intimations of Reality*, p. 63.

5. *Ibid.*, pp. 23–35.

6. I.G. Barbour, *Religion in an Age of Science*, pp. 28–29.

7. I.G. Barbour, "God's Power: A Process view", pp. 2–5.

8. J.C. Polkinghorne, *Quarks, Chaos and Christianity*, pp. 42–49. See also J.C. Polkinghorne, *Scientists as Theologians*, pp. 46–50.

9. F. Collins, *Test of Faith* (Exeter, UK: Paternoster, 2009), Film, time code: 21 min, 03 sec.

10. D. Alexander, *Creation or Evolution: Do We Have to Choose?*, p. 277.

11. Clark Pinnock (1937–2010) was Professor Emeritus of Theology at McMaster Divinity College, Hamilton, Ontario. John Sanders, at the time of writing, currently serves as Professor of Religious Studies at Conway, Arkansas. Greg Boyd is Senior Pastor of the Woodland Hills Church in St Paul, Minnesota.

12. For a more detailed critique of open theism and how it pertains to suffering, see N.J. Hawkes, *Evidence of God: A Scientific Case for God*.

13. For more on the coming kingdom of God, see N.T. Wright, *Surprised by Hope*.

14. B.M. Rothschild, "Diseases of Dinosaurs".

4 The Evidence of God in Mathematics

1. Saying that mathematics is tidy is not to deny that there are problems in mathematics that are undecidable. Some eventually show themselves to have a resolution. The catch is: you might spend a lifetime working on a problem that is undecidable and never know it!

2. Plato, Aristotle, Descartes, Spinoza, Leibniz, Kant, and Hegel.

3. A talk by Keith Ward, "The New Atheists" (Part 1). Keith Ward is a Christian philosopher, theologian, pastor, and scholar. He served as Regius Professor of Divinity at Oxford from 1991 to 2004.

4. *Ibid.*

5. J. Franklin, "The Mathematical World".

6. N. Bohr quoted in Werner Heisenberg, *Physics and Beyond*, p. 206.

7. R. Feynman, *The Character of Physical Law*.

8. J. Polkinghorne, *Quarks, Chaos and Christianity*, pp. 55–56. This phenomenon was further investigated by John Bell in 1964, who

discovered that no physical theory can give rise to the predictions of quantum mechanics.

9. *Ibid.*, p. 57.

10. *Ibid.*, p. 66.

11. J. Yorke, an applied mathematician from the University of Maryland was the first to use the name "chaos" for what, it transpired, was not even a chaos situation. Nevertheless, the name caught on. See T.Y. Li and J.A. Yorke, "Period Three Implies Chaos".

12. I. Peterson, *Newton's Clock: Chaos in the Solar System*.

13. E.N. Lorenz, "Deterministic Non-Periodic Flow".

14. This thinking has led philosopher John Leslie to muse whether moving an individual animal in the Cambrian seas two feet to its left could have meant that the conquest of land would not have occurred. See J. Leslie, "Intelligent Life in Our Universe", p. 119.

15. J. Polkinghorne, *Reason and Reality: The Relationship Between Science and Theology*, p. 36. See also J. Polkinghorne, *Belief in God in an Age of Science*, p. 52.

16. G. Ifrah, *The Universal History of Numbers: From Prehistory to the Invention of the Computer*.

17. J.D. Barrow (2001), "Cosmology, Life, and the Anthropic Principle".

18. E. Wigner, 1959, "The Unreasonable Effectiveness of Mathematics in the Natural Sciences", Richard Courant lecture in mathematical sciences delivered at New York University, 11 May 1959.

19. P. Dirac, "The Evolution of the Physicist's Picture of Nature".

20. V.S. Poythress, "A Biblical View of Mathematics".

21. V.S. Poythress, "Mathematics as Rhyme".

22. P. Davies, "Taking Science on Faith".

23. *Ibid.*

24. J. Polkinghorne, *Science and Theology: An Introduction*, p. 72.

25. *Ibid.*, p. 73.

26. P. Dirac, "The Evolution of the Physicist's Picture of Nature", p. 47.

27. B. Russell, "The Study of Mathematics" in *Mysticism and Logic: And Other Essays*, p. 60. In the end, Russell gave up mathematics because of his struggle to accept that some things were uncertain in mathematics. This idea so scandalized him that he became an atheistic philosopher. It serves to remind us that although there is much order, there is also mystery.

5 The Evidence of God in Society

1. David Bentley Hart, *Atheist Delusions: The Christian Revolution and Its Fashionable Enemies*, p. xi.

2. J. Blacket, *Fire in the Outback*, p. 24.

3. See BBC News, Asia Pacific, 27 August 2010.

4. From George Washington to the Synod of the Dutch Reformed Church in North America, October 1789.

5. M. Steyn, *America Alone*, p. 98.

6. J. Sacks, "Atheism Has Failed: Only Religion Can Defeat the New Barbarians".

7. *Ibid.*

8. While humanity may have an instinctive notion about what good is, societal culture will kill it off.

9. F. Nietzsche, *Human, All Too Human*.

10. J. Micklethwait and A. Wooldridge, *God is Back: How the Global Revival of Faith is Changing the World*. John Micklethwait is editor of the Economist, and Adrian Wooldridge is the magazine's Washington bureau chief.

11. M. Novak, *On Two Wings: Humble Faith and Common Sense at the American Founding*, p. 5.

12. F. Dostoevsky, *The Brothers Karamazov*, at the end of the chapter titled "Rebellion".

13. Vishal Mangalwadi interviewed by Warwick Marsh, Truth and Transformation series: see https://www.youtube.com/watch?v=3E5ri2z0ym8, accessed 15 May 2014.

14. P. Waugh, *Postmodernism: A Reader*, p. 2.

15. E.S. Jones, *The Unshakable Kingdom and the Unchanging Person*.

16. C. Colson, *The Body: Being Light in Darkness*, p. 163.

6 The Evidence of God in Truth

1. É. Cammaerts, *The Laughing Prophet: The Seven Virtues and G. K. Chesterton*.

2. M. Curriden, "Guilt by Heredity? His Lawyer Says It's in the Killer's Genes", p. A12.

3. I. Newton, "General Scholium", an essay appended to I. Newton, *Principia: The Mathematical Principles of Natural Philosophy*, p. 501.

4. *Ibid.*, pp. 505–06.

5. *Ibid.*, p. 506.

6. J. Lennox, *God's Undertaker: Has Science Buried God?*, p. 44.

7. A. Desmond and J. Moore, *Darwin*, pp. 492–99.

8. *Ibid.*, p. 488.

9. F. Darwin (ed.), *The Life and Letters of Charles Darwin*, Vol. 1, p. 304.

10. C.S. Lewis, *Surprised by Joy*, p. 182.

11. J. Lennon, "Imagine", Apple Records (1971).

12. World War I = 15 million deaths; Russian Civil War = 9 million deaths (Lenin was responsible for 4 million of these); Stalin's purges = 25 million deaths; World War II = 50 million deaths; Mao Zedong (Cultural Revolution in China) = 30–50 million deaths.

13. D. Myers, *A Friendly Letter to Skeptics and Atheists: Musings on Why God is Good and Faith Isn't Evil*.

14. E. Larson and L. Witham in *Nature*, 386 (1997), pp. 435–36.

15. N.J. Hawkes, *The Dance Between Science and Faith*, pp. 45–46.

16. R. Dawkins, *The God Delusion*, p. 275.

17. Exact numbers are impossible to obtain, but some estimate that 3 million Christians were exterminated, of which 660,000 were Catholics. General William Donovan, a member of the US

prosecution team at the Nuremburg war trials, kept records in 150 volumes (now stored at Cornell University) which show that the Nazis knew that Bible-believing, evangelical churches would have to be neutralized by infiltration, extermination, and indoctrination. Only those church institutions that compromised their Christian values would be spared. For more information, see Richard Bonney (ed. and trans.), *Confronting the Nazi War on Christianity: The Kulturkampf Newsletters*, 1936–1939.

18. R. Dawkins, *The God Delusion*, p. 37.

19. The women the Apostle Paul honoured in his letters include Phoebe (a deacon); Junias (an apostle, probably a woman); Pricilla, Mary, Tryphena, Tryphosa, Persis, and Julia (influential women in the church); Chloe and Lydia (who hosted house churches); Priscilla (a teacher); the daughters of Philip (prophetesses). He made it clear that men and women are equal before God (Galatians 3:26–29).

20. Key members of the Women's Christian Temperance Union who played a key role in winning women the vote in the late nineteenth century included Kate Sheppard (1847–1934) in New Zealand and Anne Knight (1786–1862) in Britain. Note also that the Roman Catholic Church published *The Catholic Suffragist Journal*.

21. M. Bragg, *The Book of Books*, pp. 205–26.

22. R. Dawkins, *The God Delusion*, p. 135.

23. It should be said, however, that many Old Testament principles were not revised and completed by Jesus, and as such, hold true today. Certainly, all the foundational principles of the New Testament are first introduced in the Old Testament.

24. B. Russell, "Is There a God?" An article commissioned, but never published, by *Illustrated magazine* in 1952, now in *The Collected Papers of Bertrand Russell*, pp. 547–48.

25. C. Darwin, in Darwin Correspondence Database, www.darwinproject.ac.uk/entry_13230, accessed on 26 April 2014.

26. K. Ward, "The New Atheists" (Part 1).

27. A. Plantinga, "The Dawkins Confusion: Naturalism 'ad absurdum'".

28. C.S. Lewis, *The Abolition of Man*, p. 81.

29. A.J. Toynbee, *A Study of History*.

30. L. Newbigin, *The Gospel in a Pluralist Society*.

31. *Ibid.*, p. 9.

32. *Ibid.*, p. 170.

33. Augustine, *De Genesi ad litteram*, II.9, I.21, trans. E. McMullin, "How Should Cosmology Relate to Theology?" in A.R. Peacocke (ed.), *The Sciences and Theology in the Twentieth Century*, pp. 17–57 (pp. 19, 20).

34. J. Calvin, *Commentaries: Genesis*, Vol. I, Genesis, chapter 1, verse 5.

35. *Ibid.*, verse 6.

36. N.J. Hawkes, "An Apology for the Scientific Credibility of Faith".

37. N.J. Hawkes, *Evidence of God: A Scientific Case for God*.

38. It is worth noting, however, that Christian truth has been fixed and stable for the last 2,000 years, while scientific truth has continually changed.

39. Note that *Who Moved the Stone?* was written under a pseudonym, Frank Morison.

40. A. Flew (with Roy Varghese), *There is a God: How the World's Most Notorious Atheist Changed His Mind*.

41. C.S. Lewis, *God in the Dock: Essays on Theology and Ethics*, p. 101.

7 The Evidence of God in Death

1. Shakespeare, *Macbeth*, Act V, Scene 5.

2. From the poem by Dylan Thomas (1914–53), "Do not go gentle into that good night".

3. M.K. Gandhi, "The Fear of Death", *Young India*, 13 October 1921, reprinted in *The Moral and Political Writings of Mahatma Gandhi*, Vol. 3, p. 235.

4. This idea was promoted by the Polish/British anthropologist, Bronisław Malinowski.

5. L. Ellis, E. A. Wahab, and M. Ratnasingan, "Religiosity and Fear of Death: A Three-Nation Comparison", p. 179.

6. Y. Wen, "Religiosity and Death Anxiety".

7. N.T. Wright, *Surprised by Hope*, p. 54.

8. *Ibid.*, p. 111.

9. *Ibid.*, pp. 141–42.

10. C.S. Lewis, *The Problem of Pain*, p. 127.

11. The scientist and theologian Arthur Peacocke suggested that human beings appear to be rising beasts rather than fallen angels. See A. Peacocke, "The Challenge and Stimulus of the Epic of Evolution to Theology", in Steven Dick (ed.), *Many Worlds*, pp. 97–98.

12. Interview with Tony Jones on *Lateline* (ABC, Australia), 30 October 2000. See also an article on the work of Peter Fenwick and Sam Parnia, "Soul-Searching Doctors Find Life After Death", in *Daily Telegraph*, 22 October 2000.

13. P. van Lommel, R. van Wees, V. Meyers, and I. Elfferich, "Near Death Experience in Survivors of Cardiac Arrest: A Prospective Study in the Netherlands".

14. J.D. McPherson, *"Our People Die Well": Glorious Accounts of Early Methodists at Death's Door*.

BIBLIOGRAPHY

Alexander, D., *Creation or Evolution: Do We Have to Choose?* (Oxford: Monarch Books, 2008).

Augustine, *Confessions*, trans. R.S. Pine-Coffin (Harmondsworth: Penguin, 1961).

Bacon, F., *The Advancement of Learning* (1605). Available online at http://oll.libertyfund.org/titles/1433.

Barbour, I.G., *Religion in an Age of Science* (London: SCM Press, 1990).

Barbour, I.G., "God's Power: A Process view", in J. Polkinghorne (ed.), *The Work of Love: Creation as Kenosis* (Grand Rapids, MI: Eerdmans, 2001), pp. 1–20.

Barrow, J.D., "Cosmology, Life, and the Anthropic Principle", *Annals of the New York Academy of Sciences* 950, no. 1 (2001), pp. 139–53.

Blacket, J., *Fire in the Outback* (Sydney: Albatross, 1997).

Boslough, J., *Stephen Hawking's Universe* (New York: Simon and Schuster, 1983).

Boyle, R., *The Works of the Honourable Robert Boyle*, ed. T. Birch, second edition, 6 volumes (London: Rivingtons, 1744).

Bragg, M., *The Book of Books* (London: Hodder & Stoughton, 2011).

Brooke, J. and Cantor, G., *Reconstructing Nature: The Engagement of Science and Religion* (Edinburgh: T&T Clark, 1988).

Browne, T., *Religio Medici* (1642), ed. J. Winney (Cambridge: Cambridge University Press, 1983).

Bryson, B., *A Short History of Nearly Everything* (London: Doubleday, 2003).

Calvin, J., *Commentaries: Genesis*, Vol. I (Grand Rapids, MI: Baker Book House).

Cammaerts, É., *The Laughing Prophet: The Seven Virtues and G. K. Chesterton* (London: Methuen & Co., 1937).

Collins, F., *The Language of God: A Scientist Presents Evidence for Belief* (New York: Simon & Schuster, 2007).

Collins, F., in *Test of Faith*, Film (Exeter, UK: Paternoster, 2009).

Colson, C., *The Body: Being Light in Darkness* (Nashville, TN: Thomas Nelson, 1992).

Curriden, M., "Guilt by Heredity? His Lawyer Says It's in the Killer's Genes", *The National Law Journal*, 7 November 1994, p. A12.

Darwin, C., *The Autobiography of Charles Darwin*, ed. N. Barlow (London: Collins, 1958).

Darwin, F. (ed.), *The Life and Letters of Charles Darwin*, Vol. 1 (London, 1887).

Darwin, F. (ed.), *The Life and Letters of Charles Darwin*, Vol. 2 (New York: Appleton, 1898).

Davies, P., *How to Build a Time Machine* (Harmondsworth: Penguin, 2002).

Davies, P., *The Mind of God: Science and the Search for Ultimate Meaning* (New York: Simon & Schuster, 1992).

Davies, P., "Taking Science on Faith", *New York Times*, 24 November 2007.

Dawkins, R., *The God Delusion* (New York: Bantam Books, 2006).

De Duve, C., "Lessons of Life", in S. Dick (ed.) *Many Worlds* (Philadelphia and London: Templeton Foundation Press, 2000), pp. 3–13.

Desmond, A. and Moore, J., *Darwin* (London: Penguin Books, 1991).

Dirac, P., "The Evolution of the Physicist's Picture of Nature", *Scientific American* 208 (1963), pp. 45–53.

Dostoevsky, F., *The Brothers Karamazov* (1879), trans. C. Garnett (New York: Barnes & Noble, 1995).

Dyson, F., *Infinite in all Directions* (New York: Harper & Row, 1988).

Ellis, L., Wahab, E.A., and Ratnasingan, M., "Religiosity and Fear of Death: A Three-Nation Comparison", *Mental Health, Religion & Culture* 16, no. 2 (2013), pp. 179–99.

Flew, A. (with Roy Varghese), *There is a God: How the World's Most Notorious Atheist Changed His Mind* (New York: HarperCollins, 2007).

Fox S.W. and Dose, K., *Molecular Evolution and the Origin of Life*, ed. J.L. Fox (New York: Marcel Dekker, 1977).

Frankl, V.E., *Man's Search for Meaning* (New York: Washington Square Press, 1963).

Franklin, J., "The Mathematical World", *Aeon Magazine*, 7 April 2014. Available online at http://aeon.co/magazine/science/what-is-left-for-mathematics-to-be-about/.

Gandhi, M.K., *The Moral and Political Writings of Mahatma Gandhi*, 3 vols, ed. R.N. Iyer (Oxford: Oxford University Press, 1986–87).

Gould, S.J., *Dinosaur in a Haystack: Reflections in Natural History* (London: Jonathan Cape, 1996).

Gould, S.J., *Ever Since Darwin* (New York: Norton, 1979).

Graham, L.R., *Science and Philosophy in the Soviet Union* (New York: Knopf, 1972).

Hart, D.B., *Atheist Delusions: The Christian Revolution and Its Fashionable Enemies* (New Haven, CT: Yale University Press, 2009).

Hawkes, N.J., "An Apology for the Scientific Credibility of Faith" (Sydney: Australian College of Theology, doctoral thesis, 2004).

Hawkes, N.J., *Evidence of God: A Scientific Case for God* (Eugene, OR: Wipf and Stock, 2012).

Hawking, S., *A Brief History of Time* (London and New York: Bantam, 1988).

Heisenberg, W., *Physics and Beyond* (New York: Harper and Row, 1971).

Hoyle, F., "Hoyle on Evolution", *Nature* 294 (12 November 1981), p. 105.

Hoyle, F., "The Universe: Past and Present Reflections", *Annual Review of Astronomy and Astrophysics*, 20 (1982), pp. 1–36.

Ifrah, G., *The Universal History of Numbers: From Prehistory to the Invention of the Computer* (New York: John Wiley, 2000).

Jastrow, R., *God and the Astronomers* (New York: W.W. Norton, 1978).

Jones, E.S., *The Unshakable Kingdom and the Unchanging Person* (Nashville, TN: Abingdon Press, 1972).

Jung, C.G., *Modern Man in Search of a Soul* (Orlando, FL: Harcourt Brace Jovanovich, 1933).

Lennox, J., *God's Undertaker: Has Science Buried God?* (Oxford: Lion, 2009).

Leslie, J., "Intelligent Life in Our Universe", in Steven Dick (ed.), *Many Worlds* (Philadelphia and London: Templeton Foundation Press, 2000), pp. 119–32.

Lewis, C.S., *The Abolition of Man* (New York: HarperCollins, 1944/2001).

Lewis, C.S., *God in the Dock: Essays on Theology and Ethics*, ed. W. Hooper (Grand Rapids, MI: Eerdmans, 1970).

Lewis, C.S., *Miracles: A Preliminary Study* (London: Geoffrey Bles, 1947).

Lewis, C.S., *The Problem of Pain* (London: The Centenary Press, 1940).

Lewis, C.S., *Surprised by Joy* (Orlando, FL: Harcourt, 1955).

Li, T.Y. and Yorke, J.A., "Period Three Implies Chaos", *American Mathematical Monthly*, 82 (1975), pp. 481–85.

Linde, A., "The Self-Reproducing Inflationary Universe", *Scientific American* 271, no. 5 (November 1994), pp. 48–55.

Lorenz, E.N., "Deterministic Non-Periodic Flow", *Journal of the Atmospheric Sciences* 20 (1963), pp. 130–41.

Luther, M., *D. Martin Luthers Werke: kritische Gesammtausgabe*, Vol. 48 (Weimar: Hermann Böhlau, 1927).

McGrath, A.E., *Science and Religion: An Introduction* (Oxford: Blackwell, 1999).

McPherson, J.D., *"Our People Die Well": Glorious Accounts of Early Methodists at Death's Door* (Bloomington, IN: AuthorHouse, 2008).

Mencken, H.L., *Minority Report* (1956) (reprinted Baltimore: Johns Hopkins University Press, 2006).

Micklethwait, J. and Wooldridge, A., *God is Back: How the Global Revival of Faith is Changing the World* (New York: Penguin Press, 2009).

Monod, J., *Chance and Necessity*, trans. A. Wainhouse (London: Collins, 1972).

Myers, D., *A Friendly Letter to Skeptics and Atheists: Musings on Why God is Good and Faith Isn't Evil* (San Francisco: Jossey-Bass, 2008).

Newbigin, L., *The Gospel in a Pluralist Society* (Grand Rapids, MI: Eerdmans, 1989).

Newton, I., "First Letter to Richard Bentley" (1692), in *Newton's Philosophy of Nature: Selections from his Writings*, ed. H.S. Taylor (New York: Hafner, 1953).

Newton, I., *Principia: The Mathematical Principles of Natural Philosophy* (1687), trans. A. Motte (New York: Daniel Adee, 1825).

Nietzsche, F., *Human, All Too Human* (1878), trans. R.J. Hollingdale (Cambridge: Cambridge University Press, 1996).

Novak, M., *On Two Wings: Humble Faith and Common Sense at the American Founding* (San Francisco: Encounter, 2002).

Peacocke, A.R., *Intimations of Reality* (South Bend, IN: University of Notre Dame Press, 1984).

Peacocke, A.R. (ed.), *The Sciences and Theology in the Twentieth Century* (Stocksfield: Oriel Press, 1981).

Peterson, I., *Newton's Clock: Chaos in the Solar System* (New York: MacMillan, 1993).

Plantinga, A., "The Dawkins Confusion: Naturalism 'ad absurdum'", *Books and Culture* 13, no. 2 (March–April 2007). Available online at http://www.booksandculture.com/articles/2007/marapr/1.21.html.

Polkinghorne, J.C., *Belief in God in an Age of Science* (Yale University Press, 1998).

Polkinghorne, J.C., *Quarks, Chaos and Christianity* (London: Triangle, 1994).

Polkinghorne, J.C., *Reason and Reality: The Relationship Between Science and Theology* (London: SPCK, 1991).

Polkinghorne, J.C., *Science and Theology: An Introduction* (London: SPCK, 1998).

Polkinghorne, J.C., *Scientists as Theologians* (London: SPCK, 1996).

Poythress, V.S., "A Biblical View of Mathematics", in Gary North (ed.), *Foundations of Christian Scholarship: Essays in the Van Til Perspective* (Vallecito, CA: Ross House Books, 1976), pp. 158–88.

Poythress, V.S., "Mathematics as Rhyme", *Journal of the American Scientific Affiliation* 35, no. 4 (1983), pp. 196–203.

Rothschild, B.M., "Do We Know Anything About the Kinds of Diseases That Affected Dinosaurs?" *Scientific American*, 21 October 1999. Available online at http://www.scientificamerican.com/article/do-we-know-anything-about/.

Russell, B., "Is There a God?" in *The Collected Papers of Bertrand Russell*, Vol. 11: *Last Philosophical Testament, 1943–68* (London: Routledge, 1997).

Russell, B., *Why I Am Not A Christian and Other Essays on Religion and Related Subjects*, ed. P. Edwards (London: George Allen & Unwin, 1957).

Sacks, J., "Atheism Has Failed: Only Religion Can Defeat the New Barbarians", *The Spectator*, 15 June 2013.

Steyn, M., *America Alone* (Washington, DC: Regnery Publishing).

Tattersall, I., *Becoming Human: Evolution and Human Uniqueness* (Orlando, FL: Harcourt Brace, 1998).

Toynbee, A.J., *A Study of History* (Oxford University Press, 1957).

Van Lommel, P., van Wees, R., Meyers, V., and Elfferich, I., "Near Death Experience in Survivors of Cardiac Arrest: A Prospective Study in the Netherlands", *The Lancet* 358, no. 9298 (15 December 2001), pp. 2039–45.

Ward, K., "The New Atheists" (Part 1). A lecture given at St Georges Cathedral Perth, Western Australia (September 2009). Available online at https://www.youtube.com/watch?v=fkJshx-7l5w (published 29 August 2012).

Watts, F. (ed.), *Science Meets Faith: Theology and Science in Conversation* (London: SPCK, 1998).

Waugh, P., *Postmodernism: A Reader* (London: Edward Arnold, 1992).

Wen, Y., "Religiosity and Death Anxiety", *The Journal of Human Resource and Adult Learning* 6, no. 2 (2010), pp. 31–37.

Weinberg, S., *The First Three Minutes* (New York: Basic Books, 1977).

Wilkinson, D., *Christian Eschatology and the Physical Universe* (London: T & T Clark, 2010).

Wright, N.T., *Surprised by Hope* (New York: HarperCollins, 2008).